The H-Word

THE H-WORD

The Peripeteia
of Hegemony

Perry Anderson

VERSO
London • New York

This paperback edition first published by Verso 2022
First published by Verso 2017, 2022
© Perry Anderson 2017, 2022
Postscript © Perry Anderson 2022

1 3 5 7 9 10 8 6 4 2

Verso
UK: 6 Meard Street, London W1F 0EG
US: 388 Atlantic Avenue, Brooklyn, NY 11217
versobooks.com

Verso is the imprint of New Left Books

ISBN-13: 978-1-78663-369-9
ISBN-13: 978-1-78663-371-2 (US EBK)
ISBN-13: 978-1-78663-370-5 (UK EBK)

British Library Cataloguing in Publication Data
A catalogue record for this book is available from the British Library

The Library of Congress Has Cataloged the Hardback Edition as Follows:

Names: Anderson, Perry, author.
Title: The H-word : the peripeteia of hegemony / Perry Anderson.
Description: Brooklyn, NY : Verso, 2017.
Identifiers: LCCN 2016055430 | ISBN 9781786633682 (hardback)
Subjects: LCSH: Hegemony – History. | International relations. | Political
science – Philosophy. | BISAC: POLITICAL SCIENCE / History & Theory. |
POLITICAL SCIENCE / Political Ideologies / Communism & Socialism. |
PHILOSOPHY / Political.
Classification: LCC JZ1312 .A64 2017 | DDC 327.101 – dc23
LC record available at https://lccn.loc.gov/2016055430

Typeset in Minion Pro by MJ & N Gavan, Truro, Cornwall
Printed and bound by CPI Group (UK) Ltd, Croydon CR0 4YY

CONTENTS

FOREWORD

Few terms of art are so conspicuous in contemporary political literature, technical or polemical, as hegemony. But its diffusion is quite recent, as a glance at the holdings of any good library immediately reveals. In the English language, the first entry in the UCLA catalogue goes back no further than 1961. Thereafter, tracking its title-use decade by decade, it appears in no more than five books in the sixties, sixteen books in the seventies, thirty-four books in the eighties, then—the big jump—ninety-eight books in the nineties. In the first decade and a half of this century, 161 such titles have been published: that is, one every month. The word has ceased to be either marginal or arcane.

What lies behind this alteration? The idea of hegemony— like modernity, or democracy, or legitimacy, or so many other political concepts—has a complicated history which belies its current wide adoption, and which needs to be understood if we are to grasp its relevance to the contemporary landscape around us. That history is one that extends across eight or nine distinct national cultures, and it will be necessary to say something about each of them. In considering the fortunes of

the concept, the approach adopted here will in the first instance
be an exercise in comparative historical philology. But the
curvatures in its usage—differing applications, contrasted connotations—have never just been semantic shifts. They form a
political barometer of changing powers and times across the
centuries.

The study that follows appears together with another, *The
Antinomies of Antonio Gramsci*, that looks in much greater
detail at just one body of work centred on ideas of hegemony,
if the most famous one, and the context in which it emerged.
Readers approaching both must forgive a brief repetition here,
in very compressed fashion, of what can be found in extended
form there, an overlap intellectually unavoidable. The aims
and methods of the two studies are not the same, even if they
can be regarded as complementary. Their accents, the product
of times that have little in common, differ more radically.
But the one, written forty years ago, was a stimulus to the
other, a connexion close enough for their publication as an
asynchronous pair.

I owe the conception of this book to the Institut d'Études
Avancées of Nantes, where in working on a related project,
a study of American foreign policy, its design first occurred
to me. In composing it, I owe special thanks for guidance
in the literature of two languages I cannot read, Chinese
and Japanese, to the kindness of scholars who can: Andrew
Barshay, Mary Elizabeth Berry, Joshua Fogel, Annick Horiuchi,
Eric Hutton, Kato Tsuyoshi, Peter Kornicki, Jeroen Lamers,
Mark Edward Lewis, Kate Wildman Nakai, Timon Screech,
Wang Chaohua and Zhang Yongle. The ninth chapter of this
book could not have been written without their help, but

none of them bears any responsibility for the errors it must certainly contain, let alone for views on many other matters expressed elsewhere in the book. The eighth chapter originally appeared, in slightly longer form, in *New Left Review* 100, July–August 2016.

October 2016

ORIGINS

Historically, of course, the origins of the term hegemony are Greek, from a verb meaning to 'guide' or to 'lead', going back to Homer. As an abstract noun, *hēgemonia* first appears in Herodotus, to designate leadership of an alliance of city-states for a common military end, a position of honour accorded Sparta in resistance to the Persian invasion of Greece. It was tied to the idea of a league, whose members were in principle equal, raising one of their number to direct them all for a given purpose. From the outset it coexisted with another term indicating rule in a more general sense—*arkhē*. What were the relations between the two? In a famous passage of his *History of Greece*, discussing the evolution of the Delian League headed by fifth-century Athens, the eminent liberal historian Grote—an associate of John Stuart Mill—argued that *hēgemonia* was leadership freely based on 'attachment or consent', whereas *arkhē* implied the 'superior authority and coercive dignity' of empire, extracting by contrast mere 'acquiescence'. Thucydides had carefully distinguished between the two, and criticised the passage of Athens from the first to the second as the fatal cause of the Peloponnesian War.[1]

---

1 George Grote, *A History of Greece; from the Earliest Period to the Close of the Generation Contemporary with Alexander the Great*, London 1850, Vol.

The latest scholar to consider the classical evidence concurs. Conceptions of hegemony and empire were 'in deadly conflict'. Force is 'what makes the difference'.[2]

So stark an opposition was, however, foreign to contemporaries. In Herodotus and Xenophon, *hēgemonia* and *arkhē* are used all but interchangeably. Was Thucydides more punctilious? The paragraph on which Grote relied opens with the first term and ends with the second, tracing a development without counterposing them.[3] Elsewhere in his narrative, actors make no distinction between the two. In the course of the Sicilian expedition, an Athenian envoy straightforwardly equates them: 'After the Persian Wars we acquired a fleet and rid ourselves of Spartan rule and hegemony'—*arkhēs kai hēgemonias*.[4] Most pointedly, it was Pericles himself who made clear to his fellow citizens that it was *arkhē*—not *hēgemonia*—of which they should be proud, and not let slip from their grasp. 'You should all take pride in the prestige the city enjoys from empire and be prepared to fight in defence of it', he told them, 'You cannot shirk the burden without

---

V, pp. 395–7, basing himself on Thucydides, I, 97. Later in his narrative, while deploring the reduction of the city's allies to subjects, Grote was unstinting in praise of the empire Athens constructed, 'a sight marvelous to contemplate', whose operations were 'highly beneficial to the Grecian world', and 'extinction a great loss, to her own subjects': London 1850, Vol. VIII, pp. 394–5.

2   John Wickersham, *Hegemony and Greek Historians*, London 1994, pp. 74, 31.

3   On a plausible alternative reading, his phrasing would refer to the character, rather than emergence, of Athenian *arkhē*, since elsewhere—for example I, 99—Thucydides appears to date this back as far as the formation of the Delian League. For criticism of Grote's use of the passage, and the commonplace evidence it became, see the careful documentation and trenchant conclusion of Richard Winton, 'Thucydides I, 97, 2: The "*archē*" of the Athenians" and the "Athenian Empire"', *Museum Helveticum*, 1981, 38, pp. 147–52.

4   Consequence: 'we now have an empire because we have earned it'. Thucydides VI, 83–4.

abandoning also pursuit of glory. Do not think that the only issue at stake is slavery or freedom: there is also loss of empire, and the danger from the hatred incurred under your rule'. The statesman to whom Thucydides gave unstinting praise for his moderation concluded: 'Posterity will remember that we held the widest sway of Greeks over Greeks, in the greatest wars held out against foes united or single, and inhabited a city that was in all things the richest and the greatest'.[5] Underlining the posi- tive valence of *arkhē*, Thucydides proceeded to confer it as the highest compliment on Pericles himself. 'So Athens, in name a democracy, became in fact a government ruled by its foremost citizen'—*tou prōton andros arkhē*.[6]

That there was a conceptual continuity, rather than any clear- cut contrast, between the ideas of hegemony and empire in classical Greece was rooted in the meanings of both. Written at the end of the Weimar Republic, the first scholarly study of the former, by Hans Schaefer, showed that hegemony was indeed leadership freely conceded by members of a league, but it was a specific commission, not a general authority. Granted was command on the battlefield.[7] War, not peace, was its domain of application. But since military command is the most impera- tive of all types of leadership, hegemony was the exercise of an unconditional power from the start. That power was temporary and delimited. But what could be more natural or predictable than for a hegemon, once elected, to expand it in duration and scope?[8] If *hēgemonia* was inherently inflatable at one end of the

5   Thucydides, II, 63, 64.
6   Thucydides, II, 65.
7   *Staatsform und Politik. Untersuchungen zur griechischen Geschichte des 6. und 5 Jahrhunderts*, Leipzig 1932, pp. 196–251.
8   As Victor Ehrenberg would write: "There was a tendency for the supreme power in the League to pass entirely into the hands of the Hegemon, and for the autonomy of the allies to be reduced and eventually annulled. That means a tendency to change from the alliance under a Hegemon into an

spectrum of power, *arkhē* was constitutively ambiguous at the other, translatable according to context (or leaning of the translator) as neutral rule or dominative empire. In the rhetoric of the fifth century, associations of the first with consent and the second with coercion were tactically available, but the sliding surface between them precluded any stable demarcation.

In the fourth century, this changed. After defeat in the Peloponnesian War, Athenian oratory, no longer able to extol empire as before, revalued the virtues of hegemony, now suitably moralised as an ideal of the weakened. Isocrates, calling on Greeks to unite once more against Persia under the leadership of Athens, claimed hegemony for his city by exalting its cultural merits—the benefits it had historically conferred on others, above all its blessings in philosophy, eloquence and education. His panegyric is the most systematic vindication of hegemony as a freely acknowledged preeminence to be found in the literature. But even it could not dispense with the telltale counterpoint of its other: Greeks should also be deeply grateful for 'the very great empire' that Athens had enjoyed.[9] Twenty-five years of further setbacks and humiliations later, pleading for peace with allies who had risen against domination by Athens, Isocrates lamented that 'we covet an empire that is neither just nor tenable nor advantageous to us', whose pursuit in the Peloponnesian War had brought 'more and greater disasters' on the city than

---

arkhē, a united empire based on domination. This tendency found vent in various forms and degrees; but it was everywhere present. To quit the League now meant not merely the breaking of an oath, but a political revolt': *The Greek State*, London 1969, p. 113.

9   *Panegyricus*, 107. After remarking that Athenians had traditionally 'treated Greeks with consideration and not with insolence', and so 'in fairness should be entitled to hegemony', he explained that if the inhabitants of Melos had been massacred, they had only met their deserts. It was 'no sign of our misrule if some of those who warred with us had to be severely disciplined': 80, 100–1.

in all the rest of its history.[10] By then, *arkhē* abandoned, he had etherealised hegemony altogether in his Hymn to Logos, where it becomes the power of the word over all things—*hapantōn hēgemona logon*—of whose authority he was the bearer.[11] In the real world, its finale was the radical opposite, as the king whom he had once sought to appease crushed city-state resistance to Macedonian rule. By force of conquest, Philip became the 'hegemon of Greece', formally installed as such at Corinth.[12]

Looking back, Aristotle would write of Athens and Sparta that 'each of the two states that were hegemonic in Greece took their form of government as a standard and imposed it on other cities, in one case democracies and in the other oligarchies, paying no regard to the interest of the cities, but only to their own advantage', until it became a 'fixed habit with the people of the various cities not even to desire equality, but either to seek to rule or to endure subjection.'[13] Hegemony, in other words, was inherently interventionist. The articles of the League of Corinth, also nominally an alliance of equals, went further than any precedent, as befitted Philip's autocratic power, in authorising the hegemon to take action against any change in the constitution of a city, and specifically proscribing 'confiscation of property, redistribution of land, cancellation of debts, and liberation of slaves for revolutionary purposes'. Even George Cawkwell, the leading modern historian of Philip's career, a staunch admirer of the king, was impelled to ask: 'Was Greek society to be frozen from 337 onwards? And in whose interests? Were Macedon's

---

10 *On Peace*, 66, 86.
11 *Nicocles*, 9; *Panathenaicus*, 13.
12 For discussion of the passages in Arrian reporting the titles of *hēgemon autokrator* that Alexander ascribed to his father, and *hēgemon tes Hellados* to himself, and variants in other sources, see A. B. Bosworth, *A Historical Commentary on Arrian's History of Alexander*, Oxford 1980, pp. 48–9.
13 *Politics*, IV, 129.

quislings to be in power for ever?', before urging 'mitigation of this severe judgment', since after all 'the settlement of Philip in 337 remained popular'.[14] Concluding that 'it is in the role of Hegemon that the real secret of the League to Corinth is to be found', he may have said more than he intended.

II

There, in the age of Aristotle, the term rested. The political vocabulary of Rome, where allies were broken and absorbed into an expanding republic whose structure no Greek city-state could match, did not require it. There was less need for ambiguity or euphemism. Nor, after the fall of Rome, was hegemony carried into the languages of mediaeval or early modern Europe. In Hobbes's translation of Thucydides, the word is nowhere to be found.[15] As a contemporary political term, it remained all but unknown till the mid-nineteenth century, when it first resurfaced in a non-antiquarian context in Germany, at the crossroads between national unification and classical studies, as Prussia was hailed by historians steeped in the Greek past, of which the country had many, as the kingdom capable of leading other German states on the path to unity. In England, Grote had not been able to naturalise the word, critics complaining of his introduction of it, and he himself falling back on a vaguer 'headship' in his later volumes. Underlining the alien novelty of the locution, the *Times* observed from London: 'No doubt it is a glorious ambition which drives Prussia to assert her claim

---

14 George Cawkwell, *Philip of Macedon*, London 1978, pp. 171, 174–5.

15 He renders *hēgemonia* alternatively as 'command or authority': I, 75, 96–97, 120. *Arkhē* becomes mostly 'dominion'—I, 75; II, 62, 65; V, 69; VI, 83, 85—but also 'government', 'command', 'rule over others', 'liberty'; only on one occasion, 'empire', if just the passage I, 97 which Grote picked out for his distinction, perhaps prompted by Hobbes.

to the leadership, or as that land of professors phrases it, the "hegemony" of the Germanic Confederation.[16]

From the Wars of Liberation against Napoleon onwards, liberal and nationalist thinkers had looked to Prussia to bring unity to a splintered nation—hopes for its eventual *Führung* or *Vorherrschaft* in such an enterprise were common terms in a still inchoate aspiration. In 1831, a liberal jurist from Württemberg, Paul Pfizer, an accomplished classicist, for the first time altered this vocabulary in making a much more developed case for the role Berlin should play in the future of Germany, in the form of a dialogue between two friends, *Briefwechsel zweier Deutscher*. Must Germany first achieve political freedom to attain national unity, or could freedom only come when Prussian military power had achieved national unity? Pfizer left little doubt which argument was stronger: 'If all the signs do not deceive us, Prussia is summoned to the protectorate of Germany by the same destiny that gifted it Frederick the Great', a 'hegemony' that would at the same time stimulate 'the development of a public life, the interaction and struggle of different forces' in the inner space of the country.[17]

By the time of the revolution of 1848, the term had become a watchword for liberal historians, pressing on Prussia a role the court in Berlin declined. Mommsen, a rising star in the study of Roman law, plunged into journalism, declaring that 'Prussians have the right to insist on their hegemony as a condition of their entrance into Germany', for 'only Prussian hegemony can save Germany'.[18] Droysen, holder of a chair at Kiel, had

16 OED, *Times*, 5 May 1860.

17 *Briefwechsel zweier Deutscher*, second edition, Stuttgart-Tübingen 1832, pp. 270–2, 174–5.

18 Adding, vice-versa, that 'the Prussian state stands for progress'—yet 'great and strong as it is, it will fall if it becomes stationary. Therefore Prussia must expand to Germany'. The other German lands had 'merely the title

published a pathbreaking study of Alexander the Great in the 1830s, followed by two volumes on his successors that effectively coined the notion of a Hellenistic epoch of ancient civilisation, presented as the vital bridge from the Classical to Christian worlds.[19] Preceding this pious theme, however, was a panegyric to Macedonian power as the creative force that had put an end to the 'wretched and shameful' conditions of a Greece 'deathly ill in its confused small state politics'—Philip and Alexander triumphing over the 'thread-bare, decrepit democracy' of Athens defended by Demosthenes, and 'opening Asia' to an 'influx of Hellenic life'.[20] The contemporary analogy was lost on few. 'The position of the military monarchy of Macedon vis-a-vis the fragmented, particularistic world of Greece appears almost as if a stucco façade on the Prussian supremacy over the petty German states for which patriots longed', Hintze would observe in his obituary of Droysen. 'National unification and a common national state figure as the highest demand of the time and measure of historical judgment. All light falls on Alexander, all shadows on Demosthenes'.[21]

---

of states, in fact were provinces': *Schleswig-Holsteinische Zeitung*, 16 May and 28 August 1848. Mommsen would later import the Greek term into the history that made him famous: see *Römische Geschichte*, Bd I, which devotes a chapter to 'Roms Hegemonie in Latium'.

19 Anxious to clear the early Droysen of imputations of a narrow nationalism, it was this religious lesson on which Momigliano would dwell, if later reproaching Droysen—'one of the greatest historians of all time'—for taking an overly political, as distinct from cultural, approach to Hellenism, and failing to take proper measure of Judaism in the emergence of Christianity: see *Filippo il Macedone*, Florence 1934, pp. xi, xvi, and *Essays in Ancient and Modern Historiography*, Chicago 2012, pp. 307–20.

20 *Geschichte Alexanders des Grossen*, Berlin 1917, pp. 33, 45.

21 *Historische und Politische Aufsätze*, IV, 1908, p. 97. Grote's view of the rulers of Macedon, from the standpoint of English liberalism, was naturally the opposite. Philip, who forced the Athenians to acknowledge 'his headship of the Grecian world', was 'the destroyer of the freedom and independence' of the Greeks. *History of Greece*, Vol. 11, London 1853, pp. 700, 716. Of

Droysen was thus perfectly positioned for a leading role in the Frankfurt Parliament of 1848, of whose Constitutional Committee he became secretary. 'Is not the power and greatness of Prussia a blessing for Germany?' he had asked a year earlier. On the eve of the Parliament, he noted in April: 'Prussia is already a sketch for Germany,' into which it should merge, its army and treasury becoming the framework of a united country, for 'we need a powerful *Oberhaupt*.'[22] In December he was writing to a friend: 'I am working, to the best of my abilities, for the hereditary hegemony of Prussia'—that is, the offer to the Hohenzollern dynasty of an imperial rule in Germany.[23] Frederick William IV's refusal to pick up a crown from the gutter of the Frankfurt Parliament was a bitter blow. But Droysen did not lose faith. His group should withdraw from the Assembly, he told colleagues in May 1849, but remain true to 'the everlasting thought of Prussian hegemony'.[24] He devoted the rest of his life to the history of the Hohenzollern monarchy and its servants.

More radical than Droysen and other friends in the Casino faction of the Parliament, the literary historian Gervinus—one of the Göttingen Seven dismissed from their positions for

Alexander, whose Greek contingents in his invasion of Asia Grote compared to the hapless Germans frog-marched by Napoleon into his invasion of Russia, he remarked: 'all his great qualities were fit for use only against enemies; in which indeed were numbered all mankind, known and unknown, except those who chose to submit to him'. *History of Greece*, Vol. 12, London 1856, pp. 69–70, 352. He was predictably critical of Droysen: ibid., pp. 357, 360. For the contrasting standpoints of Droysen and Grotius on Alexander, as of Hellenism, and the philosophical and political settings of each (Hegelian: romantic nationalism—Benthamite: liberal imperialism), see the acute reflections in Ian Moyer, *Egypt and the Limits of Hellenism*, Cambridge 2011, pp. 11–17, and Phiroze Vasunia, *The Classics and Colonial India*, Oxford 2013, pp. 36–51.

22 *Politische Schriften*, Berlin 1933, pp. 83, 135.
23 *Briefwechsel*, Bd I, Osnabrück 1929, p. 496.
24 Karl Jürgens, *Zur Geschichte des deutschen Verfassungswerkes 1848–9*, (second part, second half), Hanover 1857, p. 561.

defying royal abrogation of the constitution of Hanover—had
founded the *Deutsche Zeitung* in mid-1847 as the combative
voice of German liberalism, after years in which, as he later
wrote, 'I preached Prussian leadership in German affairs, from
the chair and in the press, at a time when no Prussian paper
dared say anything of the kind'.[25] In the Frankfurt Parliament
and in the pages of the *Deutsche Zeitung,* he continued to urge
Prussian hegemony in a German federation, and by early 1849
he was calling for war with Austria to achieve *kleindeutsch*
unity. When Frederick William IV declined the role allotted
him, Gervinus—exclaiming 'all Prussia has deserted us'—swore
hostility to Berlin thereafter, at the end of his life comparing
Prussian unification of Germany to Macedonia's extinction of
the liberties and autonomies of Greece, and Bismarck's war
with France to the French conquest of Algeria.[26] Looking back,
he reproached and defended himself for his earlier illusions,
citing his own articles in the *Deutsche Zeitung* as painful evidence against himself, while protesting that even in his paeans
to the leadership of Prussia he had always remained a strict
federalist, who had never advocated any 'coercive hegemony'
(*Gewalthegemonie*), 'unitary state' or 'pseudo-league'.[27]

In due course, the rest of his cohort would rally, in one
measure or another, to the Second Reich. It was left to their

25 'Denkschrift zum Frieden', *Hinterlassene Schriften*, Vienna 1872, p. 32;
published by his widow after his death.
26 See Jonathan Wagner, *Germany's Nineteenth-Century Cassandra: The
Liberal Federalist Georg Gottfried Gervinus,* New York 1995, pp. 162–5. In
1848, Gervinus had already invoked the possibility that an 'absolute unity'
of Germany might be imposed, in an 'Alexandrian spirit', but predicted that
such Macedonian conquest would fail for 'lack of successors to any such
Alexander and probably localist reaction': *Hinterlassene Schriften*, p. 95.
27 'Selbst-Kritik', *Hinterlassene Schriften*, pp. 82–9: written in two voices, pros-
ecutor and defendant, expressing anguish of a poignancy without parallel
in the history of the discipline. The suggestive coinage *Gewalthegemonie*
and its correlates come from 'Denkschrift zum Frieden', p. 32.

younger colleague Treitschke to celebrate its triumph. Ardent advocate of a uniform, centralised Germany, which his elders had never been, he overcame his disappointment that the Bismarckian constitution retained lesser princes and their realms in a federal structure, exalting the historically unprecedented hegemon that had, after all, shaped the imperial system to its ends, keeping firm command of its army, diplomacy and economy as no other had ever done.[28]

With the consolidation of the new regime, such talk faded. It had rested on an analogy, rather than a theory, of which it left no trace, and once unification was accomplished, became inconvenient. Prussia retained its pre-eminence within the Empire, certainly, but to extol it too effusively as the hegemonic power binding the country together was divisive. Paramount in official discourse was rather the natural unity of the German nation, at length recovered. The usages of 1848 and the turn of the 1860s remained episodic, with no continuous afterlife, even in the academy. Significantly, when Brunner, Conze and Koselleck produced their famous eight-volume compendium of basic historical concepts, *Geschichtliche Grundbegriffe*, in 1975 there was no entry in it for hegemony.

---

28 'Prussian hegemony rests not on its superior power alone, but on all the foundations of our new state order that Prussia has brought into being', he declared: 'The hegemonic position of Prussia in the Empire is without counterpart in the history of federations'. The status of Holland in the United Provinces bore no comparison: 'Bund und Recht' (1874), in *Aufsätze, Reden und Briefe*, Merseburg 1929, Vol. IV, pp. 236–7. See also his remarks on the Netherlands in *Politik. Vorlesungen gehalten an der Universität zu Berlin*, Leipzig 1911, pp. 312–14.

2

REVOLUTIONS

The fortunes of the concept would be made elsewhere. Their origin lies in debates within the revolutionary movement of Tsarist Russia at the turn of the twentieth century. In this founding Russian tradition, *gegemonia* came to be employed in a quite new way, to define political relations, not between states, but within a state. In a letter to Struve of 1900, Pavel Axelrod coined this usage to demarcate specifically social-democratic from more generally democratic opposition to the Romanov autocracy. 'I maintain that on the strength of the historical position of our proletariat, Russian social-democracy can win hegemony in the struggle with absolutism.'[1] A year later, criticising Economist trends in the labour movement, Plekhanov argued publicly that 'our party must take the initiative in the battle with absolutism' to win for 'Russian social-democracy—the vanguard of the Russian working-class—political hegemony in the struggle with tsarism.'[2] The force of this idea lay in the prospects for

1   *Perepiska G. V. Plekhanova i P. B. Aksel'roda.* Moscow 1925, pp. 141–2.
2   'Eshchyo raz sotsializm i politicheskaya borba', *Sochineniya*, Vol. XII, Moscow, 1923, pp. 101–2, a text that appeared in *Zarya*, monthly sister publication of *Iskra*, in April 1901. Between Axelrod's letter and Plekhanov's article, there must have been intensive discussion of the concept in the small Marxist groups of the time, since Lenin—complaining that

an overthrow of the Ancien Régime, whose objective—all Marxists agreed at the time, given the country's socio-economic backwardness—could only be a bourgeois revolution to introduce a democratic republic. The Russian bourgeoisie was too weak to carry this out with any resolution. It therefore fell to the working-class to lead the fight against the old order. Hegemony was not a random term for its task. For this could only be accomplished if it succeeded in uniting all oppressed sectors of the population as allies under its guidance.

Lenin, writing in early 1902 as a junior colleague of Axelrod and Plekhanov, spelt out what this should mean in practice:

> It is our bounden duty to explain to the proletariat every liberal and democratic protest, to widen and support it, with the active participation of the workers, be it a conflict between the Zemstvo and the Ministry of the Interior, between the nobility and the police regime of the Orthodox Church, between statisticians and the bureaucrats, between peasants and the "Zemstvo" officials, between religious sects and the rural police, etc. Those who contemptuously turn up their noses at the slight importance of some of these conflicts, or at the "hopelessness" of attempts to fan them into a general conflagration, do not realize that all-sided political agitation is a focus in which the vital interests of political education of the proletariat coincide with the vital interests of social development as a whole, of the entire people, that is of all its democratic elements.

Any such aloofness, he warned, would 'leave the liberals in command, place in their hands the political education of the

---

the way negotiations were going with Struve over common publications risked giving him the upper hand in them—could write to Plekhanov three months earlier, in January 1901, 'Will not the famous "hegemony" of Social-Democracy prove under the circumstances to be mere cant?'. *Collected Works*, Vol. 34, p. 56.

workers', and 'concede hegemony' to them.[3] Such was the vision
that informed *What Is to Be Done?*, which came out later that
year, and his opening salvos in *Iskra*, whose first issue contained
a scathing attack on the joint-imperialist Boxer Expedition in
China; the second a passionate call to support students in their
conflict with the government; the third a demand that 'we unfurl
the banner of emancipation of the peasantry'. A few months
later came expressions of sympathy for a couple of dissenting
marshals of the nobility.[4]

By 1904 the RSDLP had split, and its Menshevik wing started
to develop its own view of what had been a common marker of
the party. One of its leading thinkers, Alexander Potresov, now
explained that the concrete form that the hegemony of the proletariat in Russia should take was universal suffrage, which alone
could rally all minimally democratic elements in the country.
Mocking this reduction of the idea as an 'ineffectual reagent',
watering it down to the search for a lowest common denomi-
nator, Lenin replied on the eve of the 1905 Revolution that,

3   'Political Agitation and "The Class Point of View"', *Collected Works*, Moscow
    1972, Vol. V, p. 341.
4   See 'The War in China'—'Journalists who crawl on their bellies before
    the government and the moneybags are straining every nerve to rouse
    the hatred of the people against China. But the Chinese people have at
    no time and in no way oppressed the Russian people. The Chinese people
    suffer from the same evils from which the Russian people suffer—they
    suffer from an Asiatic government that squeezes taxes from the starv-
    ing peasantry and that suppresses every aspiration towards liberty with
    military force'; 'The Drafting of 183 Students into the Army'—'The worker
    who can look on indifferently while the government sends troops against
    student youth is unworthy of the name of socialist. The students came to
    the assistance of workers—the workers must come to the aid of students';
    'The Workers' Party and the Peasantry'—let us 'unfurl the banner of the
    emancipation of the Russian peasantry from all the survivals of shameful
    serfdom'; 'Two Speeches by Marshals of the Nobility'—'Taking our leave
    of the marshals of the nobility, we say, *Au Revoir*, gentlemen, our allies of
    tomorrow!': *Collected Works*, Vol. 4, pp. 377, 418, 428; Vol. V, p. 301.

on the contrary, 'from a proletarian point of view, hegemony in a war goes to he who fights most energetically, who never misses an opportunity to strike a blow at the enemy'. When the revolutionary explosion came in 1905, Lenin turned what had remained a still generic agenda into a highly focussed social strategy. The peasantry was the fundamental ally which the working class must rally behind it, guiding the elemental forces of revolt in the countryside, now on full display, to a common victory over Tsarism. It would still be a bourgeois revolution that could not supersede capitalism, but it was not a bourgeois-liberal government that would take power. In prospect it was rather a 'democratic dictatorship of the proletariat and the peasantry', the oxymoron signifying a political regime in which dictatorship—rule by force—would be exercised over enemy classes, that is feudal landowners and bourgeois capitalists, while hegemony—rule by consent—would govern the relations of the working class with allied classes, above all the peasantry which made up the overwhelming majority of the population.

When the monarchy recovered to stamp out the rebellions of 1905–1907, the Menshevik reaction was to discard a conception that Potresov conceded had been an original idea of Russian Marxism, which had played a positive role at the turn of the century, before becoming distorted in the Blanquist twist Lenin had given it, and was now outmoded. The axiom of the hegemony of the proletariat had assumed the liberal bourgeoisie would be incapable of a revolutionary fight against absolutism, but the combative role of the Cadets had shown this was an error. Rather than persisting with an over-ambitious claim whose time had passed, the task was henceforward to abandon underground work and build an open class party that would not be subject to the tutelage of a radical wing of the intelligentsia.[5]

---

5 The major statement of this outlook came in the 700-page collection,

Seizing on a phrase of Axelrod's, the Bolshevik response was to attack this turn as a self-confessed liquidation of the revolutionary tradition of *Iskra*. Potresov was now, Kamenev charged, treating the idea of working-class hegemony as merely an 'accidental and temporary zig-zag in democratic thought'.[6] Provoked into his most substantial comparative reflection on the 'vast variety of combinations' that made up different bourgeois revolutions, Lenin told Martov that no decisive collision between the landed nobility and the liberal bourgeoisie could be expected in Russia, only 'petty dissensions'. To narrow the horizon of the proletariat to building a class party was a relapse to Economism: renunciation of the idea of hegemony was 'the crudest form of reformism'. Rather, the working class should be persisting in the political education of the peasantry in a common fight against Tsarism. Far from this detracting from its identity as a class, it was only through such work that it truly became one. In the most far-reaching of all his theoretical pronouncements on question, he declared: 'From the standpoint of Marxism the class, so long as it renounces the idea of hegemony or fails to appreciate it, is not a class, or not yet a class, but a *guild*, or the sum of a total of guilds'.[7]

Lenin held to this outlook through the years of reaction after 1907, when there was no prospect of its success, to the eve of the First World War. With the sudden overthrow of Tsarism in 1917, its hour arrived. In October, one of its central ideas came to fruition, as the Bolsheviks, at the head of a majority of the

---

Obshchestvenno dvizhenie v Rossii v nachale XX-go veka, edited by Martov, Maslov and Potresov, St Petersburg 1909, in which Potresov's long essay 'Evoliutsia obshchetvenno-politicheskoi mysli v predrevolutionnuyu epokhu', pp. 538–639 was the *pièce de résistance*.

6 *Likvidatsiya Gegemonii Proletariata v Menshevistskoi Istorii Russkoi Revoliutsii*, Kharkov 1925, reprinting two articles from September–October 1909: p 12.

7 *Collected Works*, Vol. 17, pp. 413, 415, 233, 417, 57.

working-class in Petrograd and Moscow, seized power from the Provisional Government, crushing landlord and capitalist power by force, and rallying peasants to their cause by consent, with the watchwords of Bread, Land and Peace. But contrary to another of its tenets, the revolution that unfolded was not bourgeois, and overshot the limits of capitalism. There it was Trotsky's prediction of a direct transition to socialism that came to pass.[8] Not the hegemony, but the dictatorship of the proletariat, as Marx had spoken of it, defined the emergent Soviet state. Once it was established, the traditional formula no longer appears in Lenin's writing. Events had superseded it.

II

In the early twenties, after the civil war had been won and the term had ceased to be actual in Russia, the Bolshevik concept

---

8   As he would note of the time when he dissented from the Bolshevik prospectus after 1905, 'the hegemony of the proletariat in the democratic revolution was sharply distinguished from the dictatorship of the proletariat, and polemically contrasted against it': The *History of the Russian Revolution*, New York 1936, Vol. I, p. 315. After Lenin's death, Stalin would invoke the term hegemony in 1927 to attack Trotsky (and Zinoviev and Kamenev in joining him) for ignoring the importance of the peasantry in the conquest and maintenance of power in Russia: 'The principal sin of Trotskyism is that it does not understand and, in essence, refuses to accept the Leninist idea of the hegemony of the proletariat in the matter of winning and consolidating the proletarian dictatorship, in the matter of building socialism in separate countries', *Collected Works*, Vol. 9, p. 49; Vol. 10, pp. 77–8. Stalin's usage was purely factional: in his own *Foundations of Leninism*, produced in 1924 before the drive to wipe out all opposition to himself was under way, he had written (Vol. 6, p. 131): 'The hegemony of the proletariat was the embryo [*zarodysh*] of, and the transitional stage to, the dictatorship of the proletariat'—that is; had played a preparatory role in Bolshevik strategy for power, which had passed. As for the continuing need for an alliance with the peasantry after the conquest of power, supposedly dismissed by the Left Opposition, within a year of this fabrication Stalin had launched all-out war on the peasantry with forced collectivisation.

of hegemony was internationalised in founding documents of the Comintern, as an injunction to parties outside the USSR. There it made a lasting impression on Gramsci as a youthful leader of Italian Communism, sent by his party for a period to Moscow. When he got back to Rome, however, it was not socialist revolution but fascist counter-revolution that triumphed in Italy. Arrested by Mussolini, Gramsci spent the rest of his active life in prison. In the last months before his captivity, drawing on an obvious parallel with Russia, he expressly set the 'hegemony of the proletariat' as the strategic goal of winning the majority of the peasantry to the cause of the working class for the Italian party. In prison, he reverted again and again to the idea of hegemony, but in a heuristic form and with an intellectual range that transformed it into a far more central concept than it had been in the Russian debates, yielding for the first time something like a systematic theory of the term.

In Russia, it had designated the role of a working class in a bourgeois revolution against absolutism that the bourgeoisie itself was incapable of realising. In Western Europe, however, agency and process had coincided, rather than been disjunct: bourgeoisies had made their own revolutions, and ruled the capitalist states that emerged from them. Where did this leave the logic of the idea? Gramsci's response—his key move—was to generalise it beyond a working-class strategy, to characterise stable forms of rule by any social class: in the first instance, and most notably, the very possessing classes, landowners and industrialists, against whom the concept in Russia had originally been aimed. Thus in the very first entry on hegemony in the *Prison Notebooks*, Gramsci gave pride of place, as a historical example of it, to the Piedmontese Moderate Party of Cavour in the Italian Risorgimento. This coalition of commercial landowners and manufacturers, he commented, had dominated and controlled the process of Italian unification in the nineteenth century, side-lining the more radical Action Party of Mazzini and his petty-bourgeois followers, and firmly excluding any truly popular—peasant or worker—forms of political expression.

In making this sociological extension, Gramsci inevitably altered the meaning of the Russian term. For, clearly, capitalist rule of the kind Cavour and his successors established in Italy involved violence—a great deal of it, with many military and police massacres—as well as consent.[9] That was one modification. Another, no less significant, was underlined by the comparison Gramsci drew between the Risorgimento and the French Revolution. In France, the Jacobins had resolved the agrarian question as the Moderates had not, and in presiding over distribution of land to the peasants and rallying the nation against foreign invaders, had laid the basis for an altogether more organic form of bourgeois hegemony in the subsequent epoch, capable of surviving successive aftershocks of the original revolution across the nineteenth century. In France he observed, 'the "normal" exercise of hegemony on the now classic terrain of the parliamentary regime is characterised by a combination of force and consent which balance each other, so that force does not overwhelm consent but appears to be backed by the consent of the majority, as expressed by the so-called organs of opinion.'[10]

This pointed to an altogether different kind of consent from that at stake in the Russian debates: not the adhesion of allies in

---

9 Crispi, who had taken part in Garibaldi's expedition to Sicily, became the 'true man of the new bourgeoisie', when he came to power two decades later: to enforce the unity of the state, without solving the land question, 'he handled a rusty culverin as if it were a modern piece of artillery'. *Quaderni del Carcere*, Turin 1975, Vol. I, p. 45.

10 *Quaderni*, I, p. 59.

a common cause, but the submission of adversaries to an order inimical to them. In the *Notebooks*, hegemony thus acquired two enlargements of meaning in tension with each other. It now included both the extraction by rulers of consent from the ruled, and the deployment of coercion to enforce their rule. As his originating formulations make clear, Gramsci's intention was to conjugate the two. But his notes in prison were fragmentary and exploratory, not finished or cohesive, allowing for oscillations or inconsistencies in expression. In many of them, hegemony does not encompass the use of force, but in keeping with the Russian sources of his thought, is counterposed to it.[11] In number, these predominate. There were intelligible reasons for that. No communist of Gramsci's generation needed to reiterate, in notes to themselves or those close to them, that capitalism in the West rested on a machinery of political repression as well as representation. What had to be explained were the ways in which, unlike in Russia, an exploitative order was capable of securing the moral consent of the dominated to their own domination. Such ideological dominion, Gramsci argued, must propose a set of descriptions of the world, and the values that preside over it, that become in large measure internalised by those under its sway.

How was this achieved? Critical to it, he thought, were two features of West European societies that had no counterpart under Tsarism. The first was the role of culturally well-equipped and long-established intellectual strata in developing and

---

11 Italian influences were also, of course, at work. Machiavelli's Centaur, half animal and half human, had symbolised the two perspectives needed in politics, 'force and consent, authority and hegemony, violence and civility', while Croce had distinguished 'what in politics is called "hegemony", the moment of consent, or cultural direction' from 'the moment of force, of constraint, of state-legislative or police intervention': *Quaderni*, Vol. III, p. 1576; *Lettere dal Carcere*, Turin 1965, p. 616. 'The state (in its integral meaning) is dictatorship + hegemony': *Quaderni*, II, pp. 810–11.

diffusing the ideas of the ruling order downwards through the subordinate classes. These were typically the enablers of hegemony, and he brought all his comparative intelligence to bear on them: pre-eminently in Europe—Britain, Germany, France, or Italy—but also, such was the width of his curiosity, North and South America, India, China, Japan. The second difference was the density of voluntary associations in civil society: newspapers, journals, schools, clubs, parties, churches, purveying in one way or another the outlook of capital. Tacitly, given the defeat of the revolutionary wave in Central Europe after the First World War, there was no immediate prospect of taking the state in Western Europe by storm, so communists should focus on the task of first undermining the ideological grip of capital on the masses in this arena, where they could fight for the hegemony of the working class as classically understood, if on much more complex and challenging terrain.

Between the lines, there was a second reason for the list in Gramsci's treatment of his subject. From the beginning, he had insisted, in the words of his first entry on it, that: 'A class can (and must) "lead" even before assuming power; when it is in power, it becomes dominant, but it also continues to "lead." ' Lenin had led the Bolsheviks to victory in 1917 when the peasantry of the trenches and the villages deserted the Provisional Government for the programme offered it by a workers' party. Out of a savage civil war, the dictatorship of the proletariat had been consolidated. But after this test of violence, what would become of the alliance that had made the October Revolution possible, indeed of the party that had been its architect? In a letter to Togliatti in Moscow just before his arrest, Gramsci had sharply dissented from the crackdown on the left opposition in the CPSU that marked the beginning of Stalin's autocracy, and his notes in prison indicate his fears that the Soviet regime was moving in a repressive direction likely to jeopardise its popular consent, rather than broadening it in the way Lenin had envisaged, with his call for a 'cultural revolution' based on the spread of cooperatives in the countryside—the opposite of the forced collectivisation that would shatter the peasantry at the end of the twenties, putting paid to any vestige of the 'hegemony of the proletariat' thereafter. Gramsci's plain-spoken preoccupation with the specificities of the West was shadowed by unspoken anxiety at developments in the East.

Issues of consent were at the centre of both, turning his notes on hegemony back towards its classical meaning-field. But he remained a revolutionary of the Third International, and beyond the impasses of the time, never relinquished his belief that for a deeper understanding of hegemony, coercion could not be divorced from consent, cultural ascendancy from repressive capacity. His writings are haunted by terms of military origin— 'war of position', 'war of movement', 'underground war'—taken metaphorically, and taken literally. 'Every political struggle always has a military substratum', he wrote.[12] Hegemony was polyvalent: unthinkable without assent, impracticable without force. In the West, neither was within reach of his movement when he died in Rome in April 1937.

---

12 *Quaderni*, Vol. I, pp. 122–3, where he surveys anti-colonial struggles against British rule in India and Ireland, from boycotts through strikes to armed assaults and guerrilla warfare. For an extended discussion of these strategic dimensions of his thought, see *The Antinomies of Antonio Gramsci*, London-New York 2017, passim.

3

INTER-WAR

A few months later, a full-blown theory of hegemony was completed in Germany. Published at the end of 1938, just after Hitler's annexation of the Sudetenland, *Die Hegemonie. Buch der führenden Staaten* was the work of a leading German jurist, Heinrich Triepel. In some six hundred pages of erudition, it combined legal, sociological and historical analysis of its subject across three millennia, from Ancient Palestine and China to the Third Reich. In scope and scholarship, it has had no counterpart since. A legal theorist well known for his dualist theory of law, sharply distinguishing the principles of national from international jurisprudence, Triepel was politically speaking at the antipodes of Gramsci: a loyal monarchist in the Second Reich, ardent patriot in 1914, supporter of the conservative Right in the Weimar Republic, in 1933 he had welcomed Hitler's assumption of power as a 'legal revolution'.

The Bolshevik conception of hegemony had focused on relations between classes within a given state. Gramsci, when he took over and transformed the notion, retained this optic. Triepel, unaware of either, treated—as his subtitle announced—hegemony as a cardinal phenomenon of inter-state relations. Parallels between his intellectual framework and themes of the

Prison Notebooks were not altogether absent. Triepel explained that the spur to his reflections on hegemony was the role played by Prussia in German unification, just as it had been the part played by Piedmont in Italian unification that was a model of hegemony for Gramsci. Like much in Gramsci, Triepel constructed his concept of hegemony by way of contrast with domination (*Herrschaft*)—the one as power exercised by consent, the other as power exercised by force. Like Gramsci again, he emphasised the cultural leadership that any hegemony involved, and the way in which it typically generated phenomena of imitation among those hegemonised.[1] Triepel even extended the notion to intra-state relations between groups or individuals over groups, incurring the criticism of Carl Schmitt —who otherwise admired his work—for this.[2] But he drew the line at classes. There could be no hegemony of one class over another, since beyond mere functional interconnexion, the relations between classes could only be a zone of enmity, and its upshot, struggle between them.[3]

The bearers of hegemony, historically speaking, were states. What was their nature? 'The essence of the state is, simply put, power'. What did that mean for relations between the states? 'Every strong and healthy state will seek power over other states, in crude form by subjugation of a neighbour, in more sophisticated form by extending its influence over them'. Hegemony was a 'particularly strong form of influence'; or, more precisely, a form of power intermediate between domination (*Herrschaft*) and influence (*Einfluss*).[4] It was leadership acknowledged, to which the led consented. To support this characterisation of it,

1   *Die Hegemonie*, Stuttgart and Berlin 1938, pp. 2, 127, 13.
2   'Führung und Hegemonie', *Schmollers Jahrbuch*, 1939, p. 518, reproaching Triepel for psychologising the concept.
3   *Die Hegemonie*, pp. 91–2.
4   *Die Hegemonie*, pp. 131, 140.

when he proceeded to survey historical examples of hegemony,
Triepel gave outsize space to Ancient Greece—the classical
world comprises over half his empirical inventory—opening
his account of it with an extended critique of Schaefer for
misinterpreting *hēgemonia* as essentially military, rather than
consensual-political, in nature.[5]

The choice of Greek examples as paradigmatic for his subject
had three general consequences for Triepel's overall construction. It made a league—*Bund*—of some sort, however
construed, a heuristic preference, if not a tacit condition, for
identifying any hegemony; it entailed the assertion that there
could only be a hegemony where the states concerned were of
the same type; and last but not least, it led to the argument that a
hegemony could only arise where there was an external threat—
Persia the archetypal case—capable of consensually unifying
the states concerned, leader and led. The result was to tilt the
ensuing narrative in an anomalous direction, away from the
plane of inter-state relations as normally conceived. Treatment
of Rome, leaning heavily on Mommsen, and confined to the
Republic, is inevitably something of a misfit, concluding that
its expansion, 'after initial hesitations', involved not hegemony
but a 'drive for domination'.[6] In the Middle Ages, hegemony
figures only as internal state-building in Anglo-Saxon England,
Capetian France, Hohenstaufen Germany, Rurik Russia. In the
modern epoch, only the role of Holland in the United Provinces

---

5   *Die Hegemonie*, pp. 341–2 ff., taxing Schaefer *inter alia* with an unspoken
     leaning to Schmitt's conception of the political, rejected by Triepel. Schaefer
     had little difficulty in politely producing further evidence that hegemony
     in Greece was as he had described it: initially military command in a
     league of cities, and subsequently domination at large. See his respectful,
     but in this area critical, review of Triepel's book, in *Zeitschrift der Savigny-
     Stiftung für Rechtsgeschichte (Romanistische Abteilung)*, 63, 1943, pp. 370,
     380–3.

6   *Die Hegemonie*, p. 484.

and Napoleonic France in Switzerland and the Confederation of Rhine merit brief attention, before the story culminates with Prussian hegemony in the building of a united Germany.

Excluded from this retrospect are all the successive Great Powers of Europe. The subtitle of Triepel's work, 'The Book of Leading States', was thus misleading. Spain might have sought continental hegemony in the sixteenth century, and France in the seventeenth, but since they were not resisting, but posing a threat to other powers, as Persia in the time of Xerxes or Darius had done, they merely enjoyed 'preponderance'—*Vormacht*—without a following, and were thwarted in their bids for ascendancy precisely by the reactive workings of the European balance of the power, at times orchestrated but never controlled by England. Since there had never been a lasting extra-European threat, there could never be a hegemon in Europe. Nor, Monroe Doctrine to the contrary, could the United States be said to exercise real hegemony over Latin America, since any external threat to the New World from powers of the Old had long since disappeared. Still less was any dream of global hegemony conceivable: against whom could the planet be united? As for imperialism, it was not be confused with hegemony. True, it could on occasion lead to hegemony, if the conquered society came to accept the benefits of alien rule, and it was wrong to think that imperialism always required the passage to war or exercise of violence: British indirect rule or American dollar diplomacy showed otherwise. But empire and hegemony were distinct phenomena: hegemony rested on voluntary submission.[7]

---

7   This was another point on which Schmitt was critical of Triepel: "Führung und Hegemonie', pp. 513–14. For Schmitt, 'imperialism always also means hegemony', in modern times characteristically exercised in practices of intervention, whose authorisation found its archetype in the Monroe Doctrine, and exemplification in American expeditions to the Caribbean and Central America, if also British actions in Egypt or French in the Little

Behind the theoretical effect of Triepel's book, cleansing hegemony of suspicion of force, lay two interconnected political concerns. The first was to burnish the shield of Prussia. The climax of the narrative is a hymn to Prussia's 'chivalrous' conduct in bringing Germany together to put Treitschke to shame— peaceful and consensual within, gallant against common foes without: 'rising above all other hegemonies in history', 'synthesising contraries in a higher unity', 'at once indirect and direct, factual and legal, fragmentary and full, self-interested and altruistic, plural and federal', and more.[8] A second motive was to rebut denigration of the Second Reich that had depicted it, with a misuse of the term, as a power presiding over a hegemonic system in Europe—a staple of Entente propaganda in the Great War, which even such an otherwise enlightened figure as Croce could still colport in his *History of Europe in the Nineteenth Century*. What followers, after all, did Imperial Germany have in those years? Triepel had reason not to forget that time. During the Great War, he had been one of the most ardent annexationists in the country, among those still clamouring for territorial acquisitions in the East in 1918, long after others, no less patriotic at the outset, were calling for a peace without alteration of frontiers.

But associations of hegemony with violence were not so easily dispelled. It was undeniable, he conceded in laying out his conceptual taxonomy, that the boundaries between hegemony and domination were sometimes fluid. Mommsen had been wrong to say that a pure hegemony could never last, but historically speaking it was true that hegemony had often

---

Entente, with accompanying justifications: 'Völkerrechtliche Formen des modernen Imperialismus' (1932), in *Positionen und Begriffe*, Hamburg 1940, pp. 169–74 ff.

8   *Die Hegemonie*, pp. 565, 553.

become 'absorptive', ending in domination.[9] Indeed, his own construction could not escape a return of the repressed. For 'the strongest means of hegemonic influence' over another state was intervention in it—including 'an "armed" intervention, for example to restore law and order, to put down a rising' that local rulers had failed to handle themselves. Austrian intervention in Italy in the era of the Restoration, as mandated in the Protocol of Troppau, was an example. American intervention in the Caribbean and Central America was another. Such measures could be temporary or lasting, but they were equally expressions of hegemony, as US military occupation of Nicaragua in the twenties showed.[10] Fittingly, Triepel—a conservative nationalist, not a Nazi—ended his book with a paean of praise to the Führer as the statesman who, by annexing Austria and the Sudetenland, finally realised the age-long dream of a fully unified state imbued with the spirit of Prussia.

In its own fashion, and from an antithetical standpoint, Triepel's theorisation of hegemony was thus subject to something of the same instability as Gramsci's. In both cases, if in opposite directions, outcome slid away from intention: towards an unregistered effacement of coercion in the texts of the Italian, towards an unguarded reversion to it in the treatise of the German. The contrast was related to their respective

---

9 *Die Hegemonie*, pp. 145–6.

10 *Die Hegemonie*, pp. 237–40. An otherwise admiring reviewer of Triepel's book in the United States could not contain his dismay at this lapse: "He even goes so far as to deal with armed intervention as one of the forms in which 'genuine hegemony' may find its expression! We are entitled to ask how this kind of "leadership" is distinguished from the *brutum factum* of a power relationship based on pure force': John Herz, *Political Science Quarterly*, December 1940, p. 601. The exiled writer of these lines, originally Hans Herz, went on to become a significant realist theorist of international relations in his own right in America after the war. He would recall Triepel's book as an outstanding study of its subject again twenty years later: *International Politics in the Atomic Age*, New York 1960, p. 114.

taxonomies. For Triepel, hegemony was a type of power that lay between 'domination' and 'influence' — hegemony was stronger than influence, but weaker than domination. For Gramsci, on the other hand, hegemony was a stronger and stabler form of power than domination. The difference was not accidental. There was a structural reason for it, that reflected the respective primary focus of the two thinkers—relations between classes within a state for Gramsci, relations between states for Triepel. In the German tradition that Triepel shared with Schmitt, and was transmitted to leading jurists in Germany after the Second World War, it was obvious that historically, force had always predominated over consent in inter-state relations. Indeed, as Triepel observed, on the international plane, there was always a temptation, or tendency, for any given hegemony to escalate into domination, as the maximal form of power.

That was because, as he failed to note, there is an intrinsic difference between a national and an international hegemony. Internal hegemony is a system of rule by one class or social bloc over others. But in the international system that developed out of early modern Europe, no state ruled over another in this sense. The very definition of territorial sovereignty excluded this. Coercion was, of course, omnipresent as a threat—peace being merely, in Hobbes's words, a suspension of war; but such coercion was not, and could not be institutionalised, as it was in the repressive apparatuses of the state within its own domestic jurisdiction. Consent, at the same time, tended inherently to be a much weaker element in the system, as the quest for mere advantage or influence. Hegemony as a combination of coercion and consent was thus always far more difficult to achieve on the international plane, and looser and more metaphorical even when it was achieved, than on the internal plane.

II

Triepel was not wrong in complaining that outside the Germany in which he had been formed his stipulative definition of hegemony did not hold, nor in thinking that the alternatives in circulation had a specific political edge. From the Franco-Prussian War to the Treaty of Versailles and its aftermath, hegemony acquired currency in the sense he resisted: as the predominance of a single state over all others, destroying any balance of power between them—the traditional spectre of European diplomacy, first formalised at Utrecht. From the start, the focus of hegemony in this sense was Germany, and its ushers were the powers that would form the Entente against it. Ironically, the very first work to depict the prospect of Prussian hegemony in Europe, which appeared before 1871 was out, was a Russian celebration of it. The defeat of France and fall of Napoleon III was not only cause for satisfaction, as gratifying revenge for their role in the Crimean War, but—contrary to the fear of many compatriots—a favourable shift in Russia's geopolitical position, bringing it closer to the centre of Europe, which would henceforward move from Paris to Berlin.[11] This sanguine outlook did not last. In France, naturally, there was no hesitation: the new Germany was a menace from the start. On the eve of the Franco-Prussian War, the polemic of a former Saxon officer against Prussian hegemony was already on sale in Paris.[12] England was slower to react, but in due course the

---

11   V. Andreev, *Voina za utverzhdenie prusskoi gegemonii v Evrope i otnoshenie k nei Rossii*, St Petersburg 1871. Germany could dominate Europe without harm to Russia, since the latter was both a European and an Asian power, as Germany was not. The two could look forward to dividing the Austrian empire between them: pp. v–vii, 350–1, 362–3. The author, who taught in Kiev, was a geographer and historian, defender of the Old Believers and all-purpose man of letters.

12   Arkolay [Johann Woldemar Streubel], *L'Allemagne du sud sous l'hégémonie*

keyword had found its way into Eyre Crowe's famous memorandum. The Second Reich, whose conduct towards Britain
since 1890 could be compared 'without disrespect' to that of a
professional blackmailer, appeared to be 'consciously aiming
at the establishment of a German hegemony, at first in Europe,
and eventually in the world'.[13] In warning of the supreme danger
that Germany might seek to 'break up, and supplant the British
Empire', the memorandum—warmly approved by Grey—was
not for public consumption. English diplomacy preferred more
euphemistically familiar language. In the last hours before the
Great War, the wording of Nicholas II's telegram of 2 August 1914
to George V was changed by the British ambassador, helpfully
at hand, from a call to prevent Germany from 'establishing a
hegemony over all Europe', to a plea for support of Russia and
France in 'preserving the balance of power in Europe'.[14]

Once the First World War was under way, and the Entente
united on the battlefield, there was no need for circumspection. In 1915, a typical retrospect appeared in the *Revue des
deux mondes*. After 1871, 'Europe, strictly speaking, no longer
existed. A hegemony was born which, by the fatal law of every
hegemony, gradually became an instrument of tyranny and
servitude'—Germany no longer seeking 'simply hegemony,
but domination, by absorption and conquest'. But now the

prussienne et sa perte certaine en cas de guerre entre la France et l'Allemagne,
Paris 1869—its subtitle soon realised.

13 'Memorandum on the Present State of British Relations with France and
Germany', Foreign Office, 1 January 1907. Crowe, who was at pains to
appear judicious, after *pro forma* simply recording this as one view of
Berlin's intentions, went on: 'it would be idle to deny that this may be the
correct interpretation of the facts'.

14 See documents released by the Soviet government and edited by Otto
Hoetzsch, *Internationalen Beziehungen im Zeitalter des Imperialismus;
Dokumente aus den Archiven der zarischen und der provisorischen Regier-
ung*, Berlin 1934, pp. 278–80. Buchanan, the English ambassador, reported
to London that he dictated the final wording of the cable.

Reich, having succumbed to 'all the temptations of the demon of hegemony', faced its nemesis. 'Never has there been a nobler crusade, created by the logic of events and the elective affinities of nations and races, than that which has arrayed against the threats and designs of Germanic hegemony the eldest of the great Latin Powers, the great Slav Power and the British Empire with its ally Japan, in defence not only of their own cause, but the liberty of Europe and of the world, the independence of two unjustly provoked and attacked peoples, and the infamously violated neutrality of Belgium, which sacrificed itself to safeguard right and honour'. Possessed of 'moral superiority', the Allies were united in 'feeling that they truly represent the ideals of humanity, that they are the salt of the earth', and could bring peace and freedom to Europe once again. '*In hoc signo vinces!*' the writer concluded.[15] When the war was over, variations on the theme were more muted. Croce, writing at the turn of the thirties, ended his *History of Europe in the Nineteenth Century* with an extended disquisition on Germany's reckless drive for hegemony as the cause of the Great War—as a champion of Italian participation in it, he could hardly do otherwise—while at the same time lamenting the exaltation of war and nihilist activism that had engulfed so many in virtually every European country of the period.[16]

---

15 A. Gérard, 'L'hégémonie allemande et le réveil de l'Europe (1871–1914)', *Revue des deux mondes*, May–June 1915, pp. 242, 255, 264, 271. Such language was common to all the contending imperialist powers, of course: examples abounded in Germany too. The difference is only that the Entente versions, somewhat dehydrated in diction for a more prosaic age, are still common or garden in Anglo-American literature; slightly less so in French, rare in Italian and absent in Russian.

16 *Storia d'Europa nel secolo decimonono*, Bari 1931: compare pp. 324–31 and 333–43. This combination—all cultures were, alas, infected, but Germany was still to blame for the war—would become a standard trope of liberal historiography, widespread to this day. Although Gramsci had Croce's book in prison by 1932, and was prompted by Sraffa to set down his view

After Versailles, hegemony faded from official discourse: the victors had no interest in applying the term to themselves. It did not disappear altogether, re-emerging—now, predictably, as benign leadership—in pronouncements explaining the good sense of the arrangements they had made for themselves in the League of Nations. The authoritative treatise on international law, composed by two of the most eminent pillars of the liberal jurisprudence of the period, Lassa Oppenheim and Hersch Lauterpacht, explained that 'the Great Powers are the leaders of the Family of Nations and every advance of the Law of Nations during the past has been the result of their political hegemony', which had now received, for the first time, in the Council of the League 'a legal basis and expression'.[17] Such collective authority, beyond reproach of any particular national egoism, was safely vague enough. The Anglo-American powers disavowed any special status for themselves. Without a blush, Cordell Hull declared that the Monroe Doctrine 'contains within it not the slightest vestige of any implication, much less assumption, of hegemony on the part of the United States', while Anthony Eden would assure the world that the Atlantic Charter 'excludes all

---

of it, in his extensive notes on Croce written that year, he did not comment on its conclusion, observing only that in starting with the Restoration, it significantly avoided any treatment of the revolutionary and Napoleonic epoch: *Quaderni*, II, p 1227.

17 L. Oppenheim and H. Lauterpacht, *International Law*, London-New York 1948, pp. 244–5. In keeping with this conception, the Monroe Doctrine was solemnly inscribed in Article 21 of the Covenant of the League. For Schmitt's demolition of the juridical coherence of the League, demonstrating that it was not in fact one, see *Die Kernfrage des Völkerbunds*, Berlin 1926. Its designation as a 'League' had 'a merely decorative sense, like the name of many businesses or hotels. An honest friend of peace and understanding between peoples who thought he must support this League would be in the position of a well-meaning European in a modern spa who felt obliged to stay in a Hôtel de l'Europe rather than a Hôtel Impérial': p. 21.

idea of hegemony or zone leadership in the east or the west'.[18] Having served its purpose in curbing the pretensions of Imperial Germany, the term could be put to rest.

III

The Entente ideology codified in the League would have a long afterlife, as contemporary conceptions of the 'international community' attest. But it did not escape the period unscathed. On the eve of the Second World War, there appeared the work which would prove the founding moment, if a far from generally welcome one, of what would become the discipline, hitherto unknown, of international relations. Its author, E. H. Carr, had served as a young assistant on the British delegation at Versailles, as a diplomat in Riga in the twenties, and in the League of Nations section of the Foreign Office in the thirties. The experience had inoculated him against the received ideas of his original Belle Epoque liberalism. *The Twenty Years' Crisis* was a demolition of the illusion that there was any natural harmony of interests in international politics, and the self-deluding moralism of the status quo powers that had prevailed in 1918. With an intellectual range in the field unmatched ever since, covering economics, law, philosophy and politics with equal command, and drawing on a culture at home in all the major languages of Europe, Carr offered an alternative view of the time, and of perennial issues of inter-state relations.

The starting-point for understanding these lay in the traditions of realist thought that began with Machiavelli and descended through Hobbes, Spinoza, Hegel, Marx, Lenin, Russell, down to the geopolitics of Kjellén and the class

---

18 See Charles Kruszewski, 'Hegemony and International Law', *American Political Science Review*, December 1941, pp. 1136, 1129.

constructions of Lukács.[19] Their achievement was a steady focus on power, which had always to be grasped in its three-fold dimensions: military, economic, and ideological. It was through such a realist optic that the international institutions and rhetorics of the time were to be, not dismissed, but lucidly viewed. International law was custom, not legislation. The play of political forces was antecedent to all law, respect for which was possible only if political machinery existed for changing it; just as treaties were in practice valid only *rebus sic stantibus*—a case in point being the *tartufferie* of British uproar at the German violation of Belgian neutrality, serenely contemplated if an ally rather than adversary had undertaken it.[20] International morality was not a complete illusion, but in most Anglo-American versions was little more than a convenient way to belabour critics of the status quo. Something like an international community did exist because people believed in it, but given its structural inequality, it inevitably lacked any genuine unity or coherence. Realism forbade idealisation of any of these accoutrements of the order installed at Versailles. They had no answer to the central problem of international politics, which was how to achieve changes in its order without resort to war.

This did not mean realism was a sufficient response to it either. As an outlook it not only lacked emotional appeal, but more importantly a sense of the utopian passion for justice inherent in human nature, incapable of reconciliation with the idea that might makes right. In the long run, people would always revolt against naked power. The inequalities between states could not be abolished overnight. 'Any international

---

19 *The Twenty Years' Crisis*, London 1939, pp. 81–6. Could Carr have been the first Anglophone reader of Lukács's *Geschichte und Klassenbewußtsein*?

20 When his Under-Secretary 'doubted if England or Russia would move a finger' if French forces took the initiative in doing so, Grey simply minuted; 'to the point'. *The Twenty Years' Crisis*, p. 235

moral order must be based on some hegemony of power', even if 'this hegemony, like the supremacy of a ruling class within the state, is a challenge to those who do not share it', and would have—as domestically—to make concessions to them.[21] Any future such ascendancy would have to be 'generally accepted as tolerant and unoppressive or, at any rate, as preferable to any practicable alternative'. In this respect 'British or American, rather than German or Japanese, hegemony of the world' could lay claim to styles of rule relying more on consent and less on coercion, although 'any moral superiority which this may betoken is mainly the product of long and secure enjoyment of superior power'. For 'power goes far to create the morality convenient to itself, and coercion is a fruitful form of consent'.[22] If Europe itself was more likely to see a *pax Americana* than a joint *pax Anglo-Saxonica*, neither in Washington nor in London was there any sign of a willingness to sacrifice the privileges of wealth and power that were no less necessary on the international than the national plane, though—in lacking the elements of common feeling within a domestic society—far harder to envisage.

---

21 *The Twenty Years' Crisis*, p. 213.
22 *The Twenty Years' Crisis*, p. 217.

4

POST-WAR

After 1945, *The Twenty Years' Crisis* fell under opprobrium for its approval of the Munich agreement, and Carr was soon banished from the British establishment, where he had editorialised for the *Times* during the War, as unreliable on Russia. He remained an outsider for the rest of his life.[1] On the other hand, with the defeat of Nazism, the conception Triepel had sought to dispel as a polemical abuse of the Entente came back to Germany when the victorious Allies no longer spoke of it. Two historians made a duet of the term. The first, Ludwig Dehio, from a well-off academic family in East Prussia, was a decorated veteran of the First World War, who had worked as an archivist in the Weimar Republic and then under the Third Reich, during which, stigmatised by origin—a Jewish grandfather had been a distinguished classical philologist—he was unable to publish. After the war his mentor

---

1   Churchill had been infuriated by Carr's criticism of British intervention in Athens to crush the leading force of resistance to Nazi occupation before the war was even over, as a Communist obstacle to the restoration of the Greek monarchy: see Jonathan Haslam, *The Vices of Integrity. E. H. Carr 1892–1982*, London-New York 1999, pp. 115–16 ff. The British Committee on the Theory of International Politics, the progenitor of the 'English School' that still commands the field in its land of origin, took care to exclude Carr when it was formed with money from the Rockefeller Foundation in 1959.

Meinecke made him editor of the *Historische Zeitschrift*, the leading journal of the profession, when it was revived in 1948. In the same year he published the work that made his name, *Gleichgewicht oder Hegemonie*.

Dehio opened his book by placing it in direct descent from Ranke's writing on the Great Powers of Europe, whose diversity he had presented as the wellspring of the vigour of its history, and the creativity of its culture. Commanding though this legacy was, Dehio maintained that it suffered from two limitations. Ranke was at home principally with the continental states of the Old World, with little sense of the significance of the overseas expansion of Europe for the struggles between them; and he too optimistically assumed that the upheaval of the French Revolution had been overcome by the national awakenings it had produced in reaction to it, and their accommodation in the diversified, stabilised world of the Vienna settlement and its aftermath. What Ranke had missed was the global stage on which contests within Europe had increasingly been played out, and the homogenising dynamism of the socio-economic and technological civilisation unleashed in the time of the French Revolution, intrinsically inimical to the differentiated cultures he had rightly valued so highly. Dehio would seek to remedy these shortcomings.[2]

Since the Renaissance, the *leitmotif* of European political history had been formed by successive bids of the leading states of each period to destroy the balance of power that preserved the diversity of the continent, by achieving hegemony over it. The Habsburg rulers Charles V and Philip II, followed by Louis XIV and Napoleon, had each in turn embodied this drive, from positions in the central landmass of Western Europe. Happily, in each case these ambitions had been thwarted by

---

2   *Gleichgewicht oder Hegemonie*, Krefeld 1948, pp. 10–14 ff.

the counterforce of wing powers at the edges of the continent —Ottoman Turkey in the time of both Habsburg rulers, maritime Holland and England in that of Philip II and Louis XIV, England and Russia in that of Napoleon. After 1815, the peace of Europe had indeed been maintained by the concert of powers assembled at Vienna. Yet henceforward the world stage of international politics—no longer just a background to the European proscenium, but the arena where Britain was already mistress of a vast overseas empire—would loom ever larger, while at the same the industrial revolution vastly increased the levelling forces of a mechanical civilisation. With victories won in short, limited wars with Austria and France, Bismarck made a newly unified Germany the leading power on the continent. But moving with prudence and restraint, he refrained from any attempt at hegemony, acting instead as a mediator and balancer in Europe.

His successors, however, in challenging British supremacy on the high seas, threw caution to the winds, thrusting—without even fully grasping what they were doing—Germany into a hegemonic conflict in 1914, in which once again the central power came to grief at the hands of wing powers: this time not one but two great maritime states, the US joining Britain to overwhelm it. Finally, in the last hegemonic war, launched now by Germany with full and unbridled intent, Hitler overran the whole continent from the Pyrenees to the Bug, before he too was brought down by a coalition of wing powers, England and America from the sea, Russia on land. German blindness to the importance of sea power and what it meant, not just militarily but politically and culturally, was a constant in both world wars.[3] But the Third Reich was no mere repetition of the

---

3   *Gleichgewicht und Hegemonie,* pp. 200, and in much greater detail, 'Ranke und der deutsche Imperialismus', in *Deutschland und die Weltpolitik.*

Second. Disoriented masses galvanised by a demonic leader, products of the relentless advance of a mechanised civilisation, had unleashed a catastrophe that, ruining Germany, France and England alike, had brought the independent history of Europe to an end. The continent was now divided and world bisected between American and Russian power. Perhaps that itself was just the prelude to a final remorseless unification of the planet.[4]

Delivered with high-intensity literary brio, and many striking observations, Dehio's narrative left its central object, however, strangely indeterminate. What exactly was the hegemony for which states had so repeatedly fought for or against? At no point did Dehio venture a definition of it. For the most part, it figures in his narrative as the stake in a contest, rather than the possession of a holder—no use is made of the term hegemon. In effect, what hegemony denotes is simply a power greater than any other, and so a threat to every other. For that Ranke already had an abundance of terms: *Übergewicht, Supremat, Übermacht, Vorwalten*. Hegemony, in Dehio's usage, added to these nothing specific: it was a synonym that did no work. Even as an antonym in his title, it scarcely did more, since *Gleichgewicht* itself is so intermittent a conceptual presence in what follows, not that frequently mentioned and never explored. For its place is taken by something else: the *Gegengewicht* of intervention of the wing powers—not balance, but counterweight, which are not the same. The indefinition of hegemony, however, did not produce a mere redundancy, without effect in the narrative; it had a visible consequence for it, one that served its political purpose but

---

Munich 1955, pp. 49–54.

4   Though never directly articulated as such, the struggle for hegemony and the advance of technical civilisation formed inter-related processes for Dehio, since the logic of both—implicit in the phrase *die hegemoniale Einheitstendenz* that occurs early in his account—was destructive of diversity. See *Gleichgewicht oder Hegemonie*, p. 39.

weakened its historical cogency. How was the freedom-loving saviour of his tale to be described? England—had that ever been a hegemonic power? If not, how else should Rule Britannia be defined? At sea, Dehio noted—long before England acquired the empire in India at which he would eventually marvel—a hegemony could be extended less conspicuously than on land. But there was little reason to dwell on that; the main thing was that maritime powers were of their nature preserved from the temptations of hegemony in Europe. True, England's vigilance in thwarting such ambitions in continental powers was not an end in itself, but a means to assure its sway in the oceans beyond Europe. But that could be tip-toed around: it was simply an *Übergewicht* apart, not a *Hegemonie* like that of all the others.[5]

II

Two years after Dehio's book came out, a riposte appeared that addressed just the two questions that he had side-stepped, and offered answers at variance with his construction. Rudolf Stadelmann, from a pastor's family in the Swabian countryside, was a generation younger, a prolific scholar from an early age, at first in late mediaeval and modern intellectual history. Attracted to Nazi ideas as a student in Freiburg, he served briefly as press secretary to Heidegger as rector of the university after Hitler came to power, and despite differences continued to enjoy good relations with him as he pursued an academic career in the thirties, conforming in articles and lectures to the requirements of the regime. In 1936 he joined the equestrian sub-organisation of the SA, a recognised way of avoiding membership of the NSDAP

---

5   'Das Gleichgewicht in Europa aber, dessen Bürgen die Seemächte blieben, war ja für England nicht Selbstzweck, sondern nur Voraussetzung für sein Übergewicht jenseits der Ozeane': *Gleichgewicht oder Hegemonie*, p. 76.

while remaining in good standing with the authorities, but in 1938 was investigated for expressing criticisms of Hitler's foreign policy after Munich, and suspended from taking up a chair at Tübingen. After enlisting in the Wehrmacht to redeem himself, and serving as a researcher in the German occupation in Paris, he was confirmed at Tübingen during the war, and became a dean of the university in 1945–6.[6] Though by origin, temperament and period his trajectory was virtually the opposite of Dehio's, both men were politically conservative, and intellectually under the influence of the pessimistic wisdom of Burckhardt. After taking over the *Historische Zeitschrift*, Dehio published in the first number of its resuscitation a long essay by Stadelmann on the sage of Basel.

A few months later, Stadelmann—still in his forties—died. The following year, a short essay by him, *Hegemonie und Gleichgewicht*, appeared posthumously.[7] It made no reference to Dehio, but can only have been written in response to *Gleichgewicht oder Hegemonie*, the difference in the conjunction of its title signalling the contrast. Taking the Treaty of Westphalia—not even mentioned by Dehio—as the crystallisation of a modern state system, based on principles of political sovereignty and calculations of balance unknown to mediaeval Christendom, Stadelmann argued that for some two hundred years, from 1740 to 1940, Europe had essentially been regulated, in and through their successive conflicts, by the Pentarchy of

---

6   For a careful reconstruction of Stadelmann's career, see Verena Schaible, 'Stadelmann—ein Nationalsozialist?', in Jörg-Peter Jatho and Gerd Simon, *Gießener Historiker im Dritten Reich*, Giessen 2008, pp. 207–19, who concludes that he was a fellow traveller rather than an adherent of the regime. For reviews and other texts of the time that, had they been scrutinised, could have cost him his post-war position, see the same volume, pp. 113–21, 134–8.

7   Some mystery attaches to the date of its composition, on which its publication as an opuscule by a small imprint in Württemberg throws no light.

powers that would assemble in Vienna in 1815—Russia, Austria, Prussia, France and England. At the origins of this international order lay the peace of Utrecht that brought the War of Spanish Succession to an end, when Bolingbroke's statesmanship inaugurated the critical role of England within it, as the 'smooth, inconspicuous conductor of the balance of Europe'. After weathering the threat from an overweening Napoleon, this balance survived the victory of Prussia over Austria and France—when War Minister von Roon himself thought it altogether lost, wondering whether 'the sword of Prussia is not today the sceptre of Europe?'—because Bismarck had understood the secret of it, known to Richelieu, Bolingbroke, the younger Pitt and Salisbury before him: that 'hegemony and balance are not principles of order exclusive of each other, but rather belong together like the convex and concave shape of a single vessel'.[8]

For balance was only possible where a power that was cautious and respected, not merely feared, watched over it, observing, controlling and directing the dynamic of its parts. Hegemony was the name of such guided balance. Only a hair's breadth separated its benign corrective role from an oppressive domination, a universal power, and eventually an empire. But Bismarck never seriously overstepped this, and if his touch was not as light as that of earlier English balancers, that was due not to the weight of any Prussian cuirass, but to lack of their island immunity and fleet in being, and the vulnerability of his place within the cogwheels of the international machine to be managed. From 1870 to 1890, his foreign policy was a continental version of traditional English restraint and disinterested mediation, seeking no further advantages for Germany, but keeping the Russian and British empires at once apart and at peace, as an overarching dome under which Europe could enjoy

8   *Hegemonie und Gleichgewicht*, Laupheim 1950, pp. 9, 11–12.

a relative tranquillity, that he sought to preserve with all manner of braces and buttresses. They were, he once remarked, like two snapping dogs that would leap at each other if he had not held them on a leash.

But France remained a gap in Bismarck's system, unreconciled to the loss of Alsace and suspicious of his encouragement, as a buffer against England, of its colonial expansion. When after his death, and contrary to his intentions, the Triple Alliance threatened to become an instrument of German domination, France and Russia joined hands despite the vast difference in their political systems, and the Pentarchy was gone—Europe splitting into two highly armed camps whose rivalry was bound to end in a fatal collision. With the disastrous example of the Great War and the subsequent failure of the League of Nations before them, British statesmen had sought from about 1935 onwards to avoid the redivision of Europe into blocs again, by taking up the leadership of Europe once more in wise and conciliatory style, seeking in the spirit of Salisbury to integrate Germany into what should now—Russia having excluded itself from Europe—form a Tetrarchy of powers under British aegis: England, France, Germany and Italy, united at once against Bolshevism and American intervention in the continent. Chamberlain's appeasement was the only way to restore that benign, scarcely perceptible guidance of a European balance under which the Old World had known its best days. But Hitler, under the influence of Ribbentrop, embarked instead on the madness of a limitless expansion to the East certain to provoke England—perhaps even dreaming a sudden German Pearl Harbour against British ports.[9]

---

9 Conceptions confirming a certain continuity in Stadelmann's outlook that explain why he took the risk he did in 1938. He amplified his view of Hitler's refusal to treat seriously with Chamberlain in another posthumous

With this, the last chance to save the autonomy of Europe vanished. The outcome could only be the common end of Germany as a great power and of Britain as a hegemonic power in the ensuing cataclysm. At present, in the *Nachneuzeit* that was its aftermath, the French foreign minister Robert Schuman was seeking to prepare the way for a European federation based on an understanding between France and Germany. But as in the past, stability could only come if there was a hegemon to steer it. Now that could only be the United States, which might one day play the role of Britain in the Commonwealth between 1926 and 1937, when the relation of the Dominions to their Motherland was cast in the image of a tranquil hegemony over them. The nations of Europe were still far from accepting such a position, since for obvious reasons none of them was willing to acknowledge American cultural leadership. But the iron logic of a bipolar universe pitting Western and Asiatic, Christian and Bolshevik, worlds against each other, could not be escaped. 'Europe will become a no-man's-land, unless it can organise Euramerica.'[10]

Intellectually, Stadelmann's construction of hegemony and attribution of it to—above all—England, represented an analytical standpoint diametrically opposed to Dehio, who lost no time in rejoining to it. *Hegemonie und Gleichgewicht* had its insights, he conceded, but Stadelmann had failed to see the fundamental difference between land-power and sea-power, the aggressive nature of the first and defensive character of the second: England was not be equated with Spain or France, and the drive for hegemony of the latter confused with resistance to it by the former. Still less was the position of the current

---

text, 'Deutschland und England am Vorabend des zweiten Weltkriegs', in Richard Nürnberger (ed.), *Festschrift für Gerhard Ritter zu seinem 60. Geburtstag*, Tübingen 1950, pp. 401–28.

10   *Hegemonie und Gleichgewicht*, p. 16.

United States, protecting Europe from the threat of Russia, to be compared with earlier leading powers of the continent.[11]

Politically, however, the conclusions Dehio subsequently went on to draw from his historical narrative coincided so closely with arguments and phrases of Stadelmann that it is difficult not to think that he repaid silent dissent with silent appropriation. Writing in *Der Monat*, the journal of the Congress for Cultural Freedom, in the summer of 1954, he backdated the idea of Euramerica—'a great dome sheltering the whole free world including Europe'—to the era of Versailles, when American and British statesmen had envisaged 'a new kind of looser hegemony' to be exercised by the Anglo-Saxon powers over the continent, paving the way for a 'peaceful amalgamation of the forces of the whole free Atlantic West', capable of tackling 'both Communist and coloured problems'. But it was not to be. Once the US declined to join the League it was crippled and 'Euramerica dissolved into its constituent parts'. Contemporaries were warned not to fail in the same endeavour a second time.[12]

Historically, the post-war division of Europe was certainly a disaster. But that, Dehio made clear in an epilogue written in 1960 to the American edition of his book, did not mean the two new colossi were in any way equivalent. The insular culture of England, surrounded by seas and ruling over them, had always been the home of a 'free and flexible humane spirit', respectful of law and liberty, that had spread to the America that issued from it. The US, after all but sleepwalking to global power, was now conscious of its mission to heal the world's suffering, and usher in an international order of a peaceful democracy. Ranged against it was the dark force of a totalitarian inhumanity in

---

11 Review in *Historische Zeitschrift*, 1950, pp. 137–9.
12 'Versailles nach 35 Jahren', in *Deutschland und die Weltpolitik*, Munich 1955, pp. 114–15, 121–2.

Russia, where Hitler's dream had come true. There, already in the eighteenth century, Petrine despotism had shown the ominous consequences of a mechanical civilisation taking hold of a backward society, a barbaric counter-world on the margins of Europe, menacing it—as Burckhardt had already observed—in much the way Macedonia had threatened the liberties of Greece. Under an infinitely more dangerous Communism, Russia now had half of Europe in its grip. The US alone could staunch the Red flood.[13]

But though the two men shared the vision of a needed Euramerica, underlying Dehio's outlook was a metaphysic inclining him to a greater pessimism than Stadelmann ever lived to voice, though had he survived he might have made the same deductions from Burckhardt and his mentor Schopenhauer. Dehio feared that across much of the world the US was not doing a very good job of containment, as Communist subversion continued to surge or seep across its dikes into colonial and ex-colonial lands. In Europe, it was true, 'where a team of convinced statesmen is ready to revolutionise the existing state system, to avoid any social revolution', the US was fostering a new federation of states, 'a European integration embedded in an Atlantic federation'. That was essential. But the affluent society that had emerged in Europe in the fifties harboured its own dangers. There a stultifying mass luxury, insatiable materialism and outdated pacifism were weakening the defences of the West, which needed as never before to 'train its eye on the *ultima ratio regum*' of force to resist the enemy.

Yet there were also deeper grounds for misgiving. What had driven the struggles for hegemony in Europe and their ruinous outcome was the elemental 'will to live' that Schopenhauer had identified as the origin of so many of the ills of mankind, of

---

13 *The Precarious Balance*, New York 1962, pp. 272–6; for Burckhardt's insight on Russia, *Gleichgewicht und Hegemonie*, pp. 85–7.

late whipped to frenzy by the onrush of modern civilisation. In Wilhelmine Germany already, it had swept aside the lessons of history: 'The will to live is stronger than the intellect. It is the master who brooks no inconvenient warning from the precocious servant. All the servant can do when disaster strikes is pick up the pieces.' [14] In Nazi Germany, the same force had been at work, to yet more demonic effect.[15] In the post-war world, the march of a civilisation devoid of spirit towards the unification of the world had not halted, and would not be, 'unless a miracle happens and men everywhere suffer a simultaneous change of heart, and abandon the road of civilisation and power struggles, on which lashed by the relentless demon of the will to live, they are now plunging forward, for all the shudders that shake them'.[16] In his finale to *Gleichgewicht oder Hegemonie*, Dehio gave full vent to his Schopenhauerian pessimism. The historical outlook was bleak, and it would be dishonest to deny a profound sense of human impotence. Burckhardt was the best guide to these end times, in which hope for mankind lay not in the hubristic predictions of the sciences, but in individual nourishment of the roots of culture and personal life, in a spirit of edification and repentance.

---

14 'Diesem bleibt nur, wenn die Halle gebörsten ist, dies Scherben des Glückes von Edenhall einzusammeln'—the allusion is to a ballad by Uhland in which the young lord of Edenhall brings ruin to his house by clinking the magic goblet that assures its good fortune too vigorously, and breaking it: *Gleichgewicht und Hegemonie*, pp. 200–1.

15 'In the Third Reich, for the first time, one of the great nations, a nation still vigorous and vital, was in fact engaged in a death struggle', and 'when a man is battling with death, those elemental forces of his nature that serve sheer survival thrust their way to the fore with terrifying power. They push aside the more noble feelings that balanced them in happier days. Yet how unjust it would be to determine a man's true nature by such manifestations of agony, and interpret his previous life as if it were merely their prelude. So too it is wrong to stress only the dark lines of German history which lead to these latest events, and overlook the harmonious features of previous epochs': *Gleichgewicht und Hegemonie*, pp. 223–4.

16 *Gleichgewicht und Hegemonie*, p.232.

5

COLD WAR

The political message of Dehio's work, with its unbounded admiration for the Anglo-Saxon powers, was welcome enough in the English-speaking world. But its metaphysical—no doubt also flamboyantly rhetorical—cast struck too Teutonic a note to travel well. What passed into currency, its origin often forgotten, was principally his notion of wing powers. Little else was remembered, least of all what they had been held to check. Hegemony still remained so alien to Anglo ears that it disappeared from the title of his book, translated into English as *The Precarious Balance*, and rendered in the text simply as 'leadership' or 'predominance' virtually throughout, without much injustice to Dehio himself.

It would be another German mind, in the same post-war years, who shaped thinking about international relations in America. Hans Morgenthau, trained as a jurist in Weimar Germany, arrived as an exile in the US in 1937, his outlook shaped by three critical influences: Nietzsche, whose doctrine of the will to power had early enthralled him; Schmitt, whose concept of the political he had sought to refine, and Kelsen, who had secured his academic standing. Like Carr, he was radically at odds with the moralising idealism of inter-war orthodoxies in the West, and in his first book published in America, *Scientific Man and Power Politics* (1946), unloosed a cannonade against the predominance of legalism, moralism and sentimentalism in thinking about foreign affairs. These were products of a decadent middle-class liberalism, patron of the forces of nationalism which would destroy it. Behind such Wilsonian illusions lay a scientistic rationalism blind to the will to power that was the essence of politics and driver of struggle between states, as an anthropological universal: 'every man is the object of political domination and at the same time aspires toward exercising domination over others'.[1] The lust for power was ubiquitous, and evil. How then were politics and ethics to be reconciled? 'To know with despair that the political act is inevitably evil, and to act nevertheless is moral courage'. Such were the 'tragic contradictions of human existence'.[2]

In America, bombast of this sort—his friend Reinhold Niebuhr had set the fashion for it—was typical of the period, but Morgenthau's underlying message was an affront to the country. Core US beliefs could not to be treated like this if Morgenthau was to achieve the position in an American firmament he sought. Two years later, with the Cold War just getting under way, he adjusted his sights. *Politics among Nations* made Morgenthau's name, becoming a hugely successful textbook, in multiple editions. In it he reiterated that international politics was still first and foremost a struggle for power between contending nation-states, rooted in the unvarying *animus dominandi* of human nature. In the past—before the arrival of mass democracy—traditional balance of power mechanisms, international codes of morality, law and public opinion, had been brakes on the logic of a *bellum omnium contra omnes*.

---

1   *Scientific Man and Power Politics*, Chicago 1946, p. 177.
2   *Scientific Man and Power Politics*, pp. 194, 203.

But at mid-century, there were now just two superpowers, the US and USSR, both equipped with nuclear weapons, and each the bearer of a more dangerous kind of popular nationalism—messianic and universalistic—than even that of 1914. In an epoch that had already experienced total war, how was peace to be secured? Hopes of disarmament, collective security, or the United Nations were broken reeds. World government was the logical answer, but its precondition was the creation of an international community capable of surmounting national loyalties that was beyond any immediate reach. The best way towards one lay in a revival of diplomacy in the spirit of the great statesmen—Disraeli or Bismarck—of an earlier age, to reach an accommodation between the rival powers of a bipolar world.

The incoherences of this construction were plain. How could the arrival of two antagonistically messianic nationalisms issue into world government? What hope was there of a return to the diplomacy of an aristocratic age, founded on a culture of elite solidarity across Europe, in the era of mass publics depicted by Morgenthau? Why should the transhistorical human drive for domination peter out in cosmopolitan concord? The aporia of *Politics among the Nations* were in part the product of the incompatibility of the sources lurking beneath it—Nietzsche at the beginning, Schmitt in the middle and Kelsen at the end—if also of Morgenthau's concern to occlude these: the first two as political dynamite, the third as too encumbering an early patron.[3] The one German thinker he would publicly claim as a

---

3 Temperamentally disinclined to acknowledge any debt, perhaps because he so often borrowed from others, the young Morgenthau owed most to Nietzsche: see Christoph Frei, *Hans J. Morgenthau: Eine intellektuelle Biographie*, Berne 1993, pp. 100 ff. In *Politics among Nations*, he would equate Nietzsche with Hitler and Mussolini, and contrast him with St Augustine: p. 206. His work abounds with such examples: criticism of the harmony of interests without mention of Carr, word-for-word lifting of Spykman's description of the balance of power, and so on. The contrast with his

mentor was Weber, but Morgenthau was not only a stranger to economics, which had no place in his theoretical outlook, but to sociology. The conceptual infrastructure of his work was a crude psychology. It was Weber's ethic of responsibility, ennobling the decisions of the statesman, that mattered.

Where in all this did more traditional political concepts feature? In keeping with his psychologistic framework, Morgenthau defined imperialism in eccentric style as any 'policy devised to overthrow the status quo'. That could take three forms: aiming either at global domination, or 'an empire or hegemony of approximately continental dimensions', or a more localised preponderance of power.[4] Status quo policies could in turn react to imperialist policies by themselves becoming imperialist, as had happened in the run-up to the First World War, or indeed at Versailles itself, where an imperialist policy created a new status quo breeding in turn a new imperialist challenge to it. But such whirligigs were a thing of the past. In contemporary conditions, 'imperialism growing out of the relations between strong and weak nations' was less likely.[5] The United States could have imposed its hegemony on Latin America, but

<hr>

contemporary Herz, exemplary in his intellectual modesty and probity, is striking. Also formed by Kelsen and engaged with Schmitt, whose work he never failed to acknowledge, Herz was a subtler and more original mind, whose realism had no truck with Morgenthau's retail metaphysics and later Cold War postures: for polite expression of his dissent, see his autobiography *Vom Überleben. Wie ein Weltbild entstand*, Düsseldorf 1984, pp. 160–1.

4 *Politics Among Nations*, New York 1948, p. 34. This idiosyncratic conception dated from his engagement with Schmitt before the war, when he had written: 'All foreign policy is only the will to maintain, increase or assert one's power, and these three manifestations of political will are expressed here by the fundamental empirical forms consisting of: the policy of the status quo, the imperialist policy, and the policy of prestige': *The Concept of the Political*, Basingstoke 2012, p. 118, a belated translation of Morgenthau's *La notion du 'politique' et la théorie des différends internationaux*, Paris 1933.

5 *Politics among Nations*, pp. 36, 45–6, 35–6.

had refrained from doing so, contenting itself with a localised predominance.

All this was still some way short of the expectations of the hour. Could the US really be put on a par with the USSR as the embodiment of a universal will to power? Three years later, *In Defense of the National Interest* rectified his aim. There was indeed, Morgenthau now reassured his readers, no equivalence between the two superpowers. A realist foreign policy must square up to Russian imperialism, a deadlier threat to America than Nazism itself.[6] In the battle against it, the distortions of will and abdications of leadership to which democracy was prone should be swept away, for a cold assessment of the duties before the nation. Without discarding negotiation where it was practicable, these required the US to stand fast as military guardian of Europe and wage effective ideological warfare in Asia.

By this time, Morgenthau had an entry to the foreign policy establishment of the Truman Administration, conversing with Acheson and offering advice to the State Department and the Pentagon. The arrival of Eisenhower in the White House, however, proved a disappointment. Mortified he was not called upon, as he had hoped, to negotiate the installation of American bases in Franco's Spain, he turned sharply against the Republican administration, denouncing its failure to sustain the Hungarian Revolt, to support the Suez expedition against Egypt, and to stop Moscow from gaining strategic weapons superiority over the US. If the country could not plan for victory in limited nuclear warfare in Europe, was it not on the road to some ultimate surrender to the enemy?[7]

---

6 *In Defense of the National Interest*, New York 1951, pp. 69 ff., 91.

7 For the measure of Morgenthau's alarm, see *The Impasse of American Foreign Policy*, Chicago 1962: 'The first week of November 1956 is likely to be remembered as one of the most calamitous episodes in the history of United States diplomacy'—'we have just witnessed the sudden and

The election of Kennedy allayed these fears. Morgenthau heralded the arrival of the new Democratic administration with a consummation of his intellectual naturalisation. With *The Purpose of American Politics* (1960), the universal will to power has vanished. In its place, Morgenthau celebrated 'equality in freedom' as the abiding vocation of the United States, a society not only radically different from, but superior to every other, whose purpose carried 'a meaning that transcends the bounds of America and addresses itself to all the nations of the world'—its military interventions in Central America and the Caribbean seeking to create the conditions for equality in freedom there too. The United States had always been anti-imperialist. But in its fight against Soviet expansion, anti-imperialism had now become central to its foreign policy.[8]

Vietnam? Diem was an autocrat, though there was no point in being squeamish about his methods. Once popular discontent with him became too great, however, he had to go, for 'certainly, the United States, could if it had a mind to, find a general who could take over the reins of government' in Saigon.[9] No sooner said than done: within months the Kennedy Administration had Diem assassinated and a general installed in his place. But three weeks after Diem had been put away, Kennedy suffered the same fate himself, and thereafter Morgenthau—on good terms with Camelot—turned against Johnson's further plunge into Vietnam. Not that US military intervention in Indochina

---

complete collapse of the Western position under the impact of what amounts to a Russian ultimatum'—'when the Russian empire started to disintegrate, the United States renounced from the outset the use of force and thus gave the Soviet Union, for all practical purposes, a free hand'—so 'are we not well on the road to surrender on the installment plan, which may end in an atomic war of desperation?' pp. 25 et seq.

8   *The Purpose of American Politics*, New York 1960, pp. 33–4, 101–2, 192.
9   *Vietnam and the United States*, Washington D.C., 1965, pp. 24, 32.

was imperialist—it was simply a 'policy of prestige', the mildest variant of the pursuits of power he had formulated in the thirties, if a grievously mistaken one, pitting the US against an anti-colonial revolution instead of detaching it from Russian imperialism, and Morgenthau pressed both prudential and moral objections to it. They did not mean his strategic resolve had weakened. In 1967 he thrilled to Israel's blitzkrieg in the Middle East,[10] and when he came to propose a new course for America in 1969, decided that its 'most elemental interest' was the preservation of its unique position as, after all, 'a hegemonial power without rival' in the Western hemisphere.[11] Equated with empire and disavowed at the beginning, now cleansed of it, hegemony became a touchstone of the nation at the end.

II

In counterpoint to Morgenthau came an attempt at systematic theorisation of the nature of international relations from another European, composed during a season at Harvard. Raymond Aron's enormous *Paix et Guerre* (1962) undertook to combine epistemology, sociology, history, morality and strategy in a single treatise for the times. A much more sophisticated work than *Politics among Nations,* it too concluded with a prescription for conduct of the Cold War. Historically, three types of peace could be distinguished: equilibrium, hegemony or empire. In the first,

---

10 The Israeli triumph, he reported, was a transformative experience—a war that 'worked its magic' in him 'as a kind of biblical victory. You could imagine the cohorts of God fighting the battle of the Jews': see 'The Tragedy of the German Jewish Intellectual', in Bernard Rosenberg and Ernest Goldstein, *Creators and Disturbers: Reminiscences by Jewish Intellectuals of New York,* New York 1982, pp. 78–9.

11 *A New Foreign Policy for the United States,* New York 1969, p. 156.

the strength of states was in balance; in the second, one state dominated all others; in the third, one state outclassed all others, to the point of absorbing them.[12] None of these, however, really applied to the Cold War. They were defined by distributions of power, whereas the confrontation between the West and the Soviet Union was best characterised as a peace by terror, since in the nuclear age each could strike a mortal blow at the other, creating a limit-condition of mutual impotence. That did not mean, in any way, that the two forces in conflict were homogeneous, or that the only safe future lay in an accommodation between them.

Taking Morgenthau to task on both counts, Aron charged him with reproducing an amoralism traceable back to Treitschke, in treating the foreign policy of all states as basically of the same nature. This was to efface the vast moral and political difference between the democracies of the West and the totalitarianism of the East. Diplomacy could not be divorced from ideology: the Communist powers certainly did not separate the two, and the West should not either. Moreover, in the struggle against totalitarianism, prudence was not to be confused with moderation or compromise in all circumstances. The goal of the democracies in the Cold War could not be just to avoid thermonuclear disaster. It should be victory over the adversary.[13] Defence and illustration of the West required no less.

---

12 Aron reproducing Triepel's index of the latter, without knowing it: *Paix et guerre entre les nations*, Paris 1962, p. 158.

13 *Paix et guerre entre les nations*, p. 654. He added 'or not be vanquished'. There was no need to conceive victory in the spirit of Cato. The aim of the West should be just to destroy the Soviet regime, so long as it aimed at a universal diffusion of what it called socialism, rather than the USSR itself. After 1945, decisive action could have prevented the communisation of Eastern Europe, and in 1956 might have liberated Hungary. But so long as it kept up its military guard, the ideological superiority of the West would now suffice for the purpose: 'to survive is to win': pp. 665, 686–7.

Among Aron's many gifts was not—in this, typical of his formation—careful reading of authors.[14] By the time he published *Paix et Guerre*, Morgenthau had long moved on to common ground with him. In the duet between the two, it was Aron who would proceed in the seventies to repeat unawares some of the misgivings of Morgenthau in the fifties. Offering a survey of the history of American foreign policy since the War, *République imperial* (1973) sought to dispel misunderstandings to which its title might give rise by parsing its adjective and distinguishing its object from seeming adjacent conceptions. 'Empire' connoted 'the more or less irresistible ability of a state to impose its will should it need to', and 'imperialist' was a pejorative term. 'Imperial' described something else: its association was with glory, rather than force. The American republic had not become an empire, and its foreign policy could not generally be termed imperialist. 'Hegemony', on the other hand, was a legitimate description of its political role in Europe, whose democracies it protected from invasion by the Soviet Union. In the Atlantic alliance, 'the United States exercised hegemony in the true sense, or what the Americans themselves call "leadership".'[15]

In the Caribbean, by contrast, US foreign policy had admittedly been imperialist. But this was an exception. Elsewhere

---

14 Aron's linkage of Morgenthau to Treitschke was far off the mark. Though himself on the best of terms with Schmitt, who congratulated him warmly on *Paix et guerre*, he was plainly unaware of Morgenthau's debt to him: philological precision was not his forte. Morgenthau, naturally nettled by Aron's treatment of him, replied in kind with a dismissive notice of *Paix et guerre*. His depiction in an earlier piece of Aron as an impressionist was, if only in this respect, not wrong, though Morgenthau himself was still more cavalier with his sources: 'Foreign Policy: the Conservative School', *World Politics*, January 1955, pp. 284–6, and *American Political Science Review*, December 1967, pp. 1110–12.

15 *République impérial. Les États-Unis dans le monde, 1945–1972*, Paris 1973, pp. 260–4, 176.

its diplomacy could certainly be termed imperial, in the sense that it intervened all over the world, without constructing an empire; but that was more or less true of any great power in its traditional nineteenth century sense. All inter-state systems throughout history had been hierarchical, and if the influence of great powers on the domestic affairs and foreign conduct of smaller countries were to be called imperialism, then like Descartes' *bon sens*, it had never been so widely shared as today. There remained, it was true, a particular question: what was the relationship between the military power of the United States and capitalist expansion? 'Is the United States defending the free world or a world open to a free economy?' [16] It was difficult to answer this categorically, since the two objectives tended to merge into each other. America had not always protected countries with liberal institutions, and had sometimes supported dictatorships as a barrier to communism. It was also plausible that in the absence of US military supremacy, other countries would not have consented to the privilege of the dollar in the international monetary system, lending Washington the foreign currency it needed to police the world. But in an overall perspective, the ultimate aim of American diplomacy was simply to contain the spread of Communism, while the presence of American troops created the moral and political climate in which the economies of Western Europe and Japan had flourished for half a century.[17]

Was all well, therefore, in the free world? Regrettably, there were grounds for unease. In the preface to the American edition of his book, which appeared in early 1974, Aron declared: 'I feel that for once I can speak forthrightly and assert that it is on Richard Nixon and Henry Kissinger that a European pins his

---

16 *République imperial,* pp. 187 ff.
17 *République impérial,* pp. 214, 317.

hopes for a foreign policy governed by reason.' But a European could also harbour some fears, at once for them and about them. Even if 'few sensible persons, it seems to me, would accuse the President himself of being cognizant of or ordering the break-in and bugging of the Democratic Party's headquarters', Watergate was sapping the ability of the White House to conduct a strong foreign policy. Disquieting, too, was Nixon's 'strange and absurd definition of an ideal peace' based on a confused notion of an even balance of powers in a multi-polar world. Noticeable was his insistence on the words 'restraint' and 'self-restraint' in a report to Congress, which occurred more frequently than any other terms.[18] Prudence was an Aristotelian virtue, no doubt. But was US diplomacy becoming no more than 'negatively ideological', limited to preventing further Marxist-Leninist parties from coming to power? In the twentieth century, Aron reminded his readers, he had written that 'the strength of a great power is diminished if it ceases to serve a great idea'. Was détente not in danger of losing sight of that? The popular and intellectual mood in America after Nixon's visit to China and the winding-up of the Vietnam War showed worrying signs of neo-isolationism. America could not afford any sulking in its tent. It was the champion in the play of inter-state relations, and 'the title-holder must constantly put his title to the test'.[19]

Ending on this agonistic note, Aron's plea for the role of the United States in the world, not unlike Morgenthau's before him, risked unravelling its definitions. American hegemony was leadership in the Cold War, not command. But its ultimate aim should be victory. Forgotten was his dictum, early in *Paix*

18 *The Imperial Republic: The United States and the World, 1945–1973*, Engle-wood Cliffs, 1974, pp. ix–x, 156, 161: passages added to the American edition.

19 *République impérial*, pp. 305, 327–8.

et Guerre, that 'since history offers few examples of hegemonic states that do not abuse their force, a state to which victory gives hegemony will be deemed an aggressor, whatever the intentions of those governing it',[20] a judgment of which the next century would supply its illustrations.

Morgenthau and Aron were writing during and about the high Cold War. Virtually exact contemporaries, they were Europeans who could remember the First World War and were formed by the world of Versailles. Hegemony belonged to an inherited vocabulary, surfacing at different points in their writing without undue emphasis: neither omissible, nor central, in constructions focused on a bipolar international order remote from the inter-state system of the Belle Epoque or Locarno, and devoted to the battle of freedom against totalitarianism. Its significations could be adjusted to local purposes in an overall argument whose general direction lay elsewhere.

For the time being, tighter usage and more direct focus would be rare and come only from study of an older world. Shortly before *République impérial* appeared, a solitary American political scientist, Charles Doran, published a work still more premonitory of problems of the next century, entitled *The Politics of Assimilation: Hegemony and Its Aftermath*, which looked at the response to successive bids for hegemony in Europe—Habsburg, Bourbon, Napoleonic—and not only how they were dismantled—by subjugation, negotiation and maintenance of order, at Westphalia, Utrecht and Vienna—but the outcome of these settlements. Empire and hegemony were inseparable concepts. The distinction between them lay in the types of control they exercised over those subject to them: formal and less formal, direct and more indirect. Hegemony was not peaceful. Armed force was its principal constituent,

---

20 *Paix et Guerre*, p. 94.

and military expansion its natural path. 'Assimilation' of a hegemon—first its defeat and then its absorption in a pacified order—required superior armed force, and then political skill; and from among the victors could emerge a future hegemon wreaking the greatest destruction on the order so created.[21] Neither of the leading strategic thinkers of the time noticed this coda to their work.

21 *The Politics of Assimilation: Hegemony and Its Aftermath*, Baltimore 1971, pp. 20, 202–3.

6

AMERICANA

The new period that began in 1973, shortly after Aron finished his manuscript on the imperial republic, altered these coordinates. The end of Bretton Woods, defeat in Vietnam, and the oil embargo, not to speak of domestic political turmoil, led to a sudden *Gestalt* switch, that for the first time made hegemony a central issue of theoretical and political debate in the US. The precipitant of the change, unintended and indeed unwanted by its originator, was the appearance of a work of economic history. Charles Kindleberger's *World in Depression 1929–1939* argued that the fundamental reason for the prolonged slump of the thirties lay in the inability of Britain any longer, and the unwillingness of the United States as yet, to assume the responsibility of providing the international economy with the means necessary to stabilise it in a crisis—a market for distress goods, a steady flow of capital, and a mechanism for assuring liquidity in an emergency. These were public goods, Kindleberger explained, which benefitted all, even if they involved a certain burden to the state which supplied them. That meant leadership. Victorian Britain had provided this, and the United States had learnt to do so after the Second World War. Now, however—he was writing in 1973, after the dollar had been cut free from gold by Nixon—US leadership was slipping away. Kindleberger did not enlarge on this opinion, briefly evoked only in the last two pages of his book. But the conjuncture worked to amplify it.

Three years earlier, Stanley Hoffmann, born in Austria and educated in France, Aron's closest friend in America, had published an article in the journal *International Organization* in which he observed that world politics was becoming increasingly penetrated by transnational society, whose institutions and agents—multi-national corporations were an obvious case—had rules of their own, which states had to respect on pain of costs to themselves. The result was to multiply the number of chessboards—no longer confined to diplomacy and war, but including trade, finance, aid, space research, culture—on which competition between states was now played. This was a hopeful development, since these chessboards did not entail the use of force, and so reduced the likelihood of overt conflict between states, increasing the attractions for them of cooperation or bargaining instead.[1] Promptly, two pupils of Hoffmann produced a special number of the same journal devoted to 'Transnational Relations and World Politics'. Announcing that they were seeking to 'challenge basic assumptions that underlie the analysis of international relations', its editors Robert Keohane and Joseph Nye argued that the study of world politics needed to get away from the state-centric paradigm exemplified by Morgenthau and Aron, and turn its attention to the intercourse of non-governmental organisations and relationships.[2] A

---

1 'International Organization and the International System', *International Organization*, Summer 1970, pp. 389–413.

2 'Introduction', *International Organization*, Summer 1971, pp. 329–49. Four hundred pages of articles followed, covering everything from economics to science, religion to space, peace to revolution, but with a pronounced tilt to business of one kind or another, generating much the largest group of texts.

sensitive understanding of these was essential for the normative pursuit of peace, democracy, welfare and justice.

In this eirenic prospectus, one dissonant note was struck. The collection's contributor on the multi-national corporation, Robert Gilpin, did not think its activities were significantly independent of the states in which they were based, nor that the increasing interdependence of national economies meant that the role of governments in economic life was decreasing, but rather the reverse. In illustrating his case, expanded in his book *US Power and the Multinational Corporation* (1975), Gilpin freely referred to British and American hegemony. For their part Keohane and Nye, returning to the charge with *Power and Interdependence. World Politics in Transition* (1977), set out to show that such a notion was misleading or irrelevant to the ways in which rules of 'complex interdependence' in such areas as oceans and money had evolved, where 'international regimes' had emerged that were not the product of any one dominant power. Soon afterwards, Keohane took extended aim at what he dubbed 'hegemonic stability theory', the notion that a strong international economic system required a hegemonic power to lend it coherence and resilience, singling Kindleberger and Gilpin out for criticism. Experience showed, on the contrary, that a hegemon was neither a necessary nor a sufficient condition of a stable economic order, alterations in which could not be readily correlated with shifts in political power.[3] Four years later Keohane offered his full-stretch alternative account in *After Hegemony*. If the post-war United States had possessed an ability to set the essential rules of inter-state relations in the matters of trade, finance and petroleum, this ascendancy had

---

3 'The Theory of Hegemonic Stability and Changes in International Economic Regimes, 1967–1977', in Ole Holsti, Randolph Siverson and Alexander George (eds), *Change in the International System*, Boulder 1980, pp. 131–62, amplifying *Power and Interdependence*, Boston 1977, pp. 42–9.

faded after the mid-sixties, as the relative weight of its economy declined with the rise of Western Europe and Japan. Yet no major disruptions ensued in a world where international relations were no longer a zero-sum struggle for ascendancy, but essentially a positive-sum system of economic exchanges, in which states negotiated with each other over tariffs and regulations to arrive at mutually advantageous bargains, sustaining international regimes that were peaceful and consensual, where no single state could lord it over others. The United States was now just a partner, albeit a large one, in a new multilateral order founded on reciprocal adjustment and rational cooperation.

Kindleberger was having none of this. For Keohane, the role played by the US after the war met the description of hegemony, but was no longer required. For Kindleberger, it was the other way round; the term was unacceptable, but the function was indispensable. Hegemony was 'a word that makes me uncomfortable because of its overtones of force, threat, pressure.' Not hegemony, but leadership was needed, and 'I think it is possible to lead without arm-twisting, to act responsibly without pushing and shoving other countries.'[4] Keohane's belief that international

<hr/>

4   'Hierarchy versus inertial cooperation', *International Organization*, Autumn 1986, pp. 841–2. Kindleberger had forgotten that elsewhere he had written: 'Leadership may be thought of at first blush as persuading others to follow a course of action which might not be in the follower's short-run interest if it were truly independent. As will be suggested below, it has strong elements of both arm-twisting and bribery. Without it, however, there may be an inadequate amount of public goods produced': see 'Dominance and Leadership in the International Economy', *International Studies Quarterly*, June 1981, p. 243. In this article, Kindleberger made clear his debt to the work of François Perroux: 'Dominance was a concept introduced into economic discussion, especially French economic discussion, by François Perroux. One country, firm, or person dominated another when the other had to take account of what the first entity did, but the first could equally ignore the second. It was a peculiarly French idea, with strong overtones of resentment at alleged domination by the United States in fields of foreign

public goods could be produced without a strong power—'a so-called "hegemon"'—providing such leadership was an illusion, and his book had been obliged to resort to a veritable treasure-trove of safety clauses to maintain otherwise. 'I am a realist when it comes to regimes', he declared[5]—if a euphemist when it came to describing them.

II

Hegemony, as for the first time it became naturalised in American political science, thus acquired—unlike any previous version—an essentially economic field of meaning, the least likely to ruffle native liberal sensibility. Commerce, currency, commodities were the domains where, in stability theory, hegemony was either operative or absent: transactions without taint of force, as Hoffman had noted. He himself could not follow his pupils all the way onto the sunlit plateau of complex interdependence. Aron stood in the way of that: diplomacy and war could not be shunted aside. But nor could they be taken as analytically so decisive as in the past. The *classiques* had believed that the pursuit of power in conditions of generalised insecurity was the overriding imperative for all states. The *modernes*

---

exchange, trade policy, multinational enterprise and the like', and to that degree uncomfortable for Kindleberger, notwithstanding his admission of the need for arm-twisting. Perroux himself, in launching his concept and noting its bearing on the position of the United States in the world economy after 1945, had described it as a work of pure science, that eschewed any 'sterile polemics' or 'explosive vocabulary', especially any 'emotional talk' of imperialism. Nevertheless, his conclusion that a dominant economy which had not suffered from the war might 'benefit from an immense "collective" rent', was bound to make his younger American colleague uneasy. See 'Esquisse d'une théorie de l'économie dominante', *Économie appliquée*, Vol. 1, 1948, pp. 246, 269, 283.

5 'International Public Goods without International Government', *American Economic Review*, March 1986, pp. 8, 11.

contended that the objectives of economic growth and domestic welfare had displaced it. Hoffmann swayed between the two. The result was an intellectual hybrid. The Cold War could not be described simply as a conflict between the two superpowers, because the postwar economic system was 'not a bipolar, but a hegemonic order', in which the position of the United States could be compared to that of Britain a century earlier, whose dominance was not purely exploitative, resting simply on material preponderance, but gave other nations grounds for taking part in the system. This order was indeed passing, but a harmonious regime of interdependence had not yet replaced it. Plenty of neo-mercantilism obstructed that. Economic development, and even cooperation where it existed, was not pacifying the world. Nuclear war might seem remote, but military security remained the ultimate concern of every state, in a time in which poor countries showed less reluctance than rich to proceed to arms.

In these dangerous conditions, needed was a 'world order in which violence and economic disruptions were tamed', whose formula should be 'moderation plus'. American hegemony was over, and the US should conduct itself in a spirit of 'modesty plus'. That required a new foreign policy elite. But the country could not shed its responsibilities. Hoffman entitled his book *Primacy or World Order*, but its underlying message was that if it steered the right course, the US could have both. 'Leadership without hegemony' was the right way forward.[6] In this replication of Kindleberger's preference for the one and *pudeur* towards the other, as in Hoffman's construction as a whole, hegemony had undergone a slippage of meaning. At first confined to economic relations within the Atlantic community, it had tacitly

---

6   *Primacy or World Order: American Foreign Policy since the Cold War*, New York 1978, pp. 13–14, 151–61, 188, 208.

reverted to a general dominance in the world at large, without conceptual resolution. The weak term 'primacy', neither motivated nor actually employed in the book itself, was the token of an evasion.

Three years later, the American debate was lifted to another plane by Gilpin, whose *War and Change in World Politics* broke as cleanly with what had gone before as Carr—his most important inspiration—had done in Britain at the end of the thirties. Here military, economic and cultural forms of power were unified in an analytic of hegemony conceived dynamically, in an international system governed by differential growth in the power of the states composing it. In periods of equilibrium, the power and prestige of the dominant states ensured the submission of lesser ones to them—prestige, as Carr had written, being the equivalent of authority in domestic politics, and as such the everyday currency of international relations, making resort to violence unnecessary. Periods of peace and stability were those where its rank-order was clear and unchallenged. Structural crises arose when there was a disjuncture between the hierarchy of prestige, division of territory, economic position, legal or informal rules of the system—reflecting the interests of the dominant state or states—and underlying transformations in the distribution of power, with the emergence of an increasingly strong rival or rivals to them. Such crises were typically resolved in hegemonic wars for control of the system, and successive hegemonies formed the fundamental ordering principle of international relations. As Gilpin noted, this had been the view of Lenin and Trotsky—uneven and combined development as the cordite for explosions between the great powers. 'A theory of international political change must of necessity also be a theory of imperialism and political integration.'[7]

---

7   *War and Change in World Politics*, Cambridge 1981, pp. 13–15, 23, 31.

Modern states did not seek to maximise either power or welfare (on which domestic stability depended), as Hoffman's antithesis suggested, but to optimise their different objectives, as on a set of indifference curves. Economic growth was a condition of both military strength and popular satisfaction, requirements for any hegemon. But hegemony eventually took its toll. Typically, protection costs increased as the extent of imperial control expanded. Accustomed wealth led to an increase in the share of consumption in national income, and a fall in that of investment. Diffusion of economic, technological and organisational skills undermined the competitive edge of the hegemon, newer states enjoying lower costs, rising profits and the advantages of backwardness. Last but not least, blind self-satisfaction and belief in the natural rightness of dominion became habitual. There were signs of all these symptoms of decline in the United States. The costs of governing the system had risen relative to its economic capacity to enforce the international status quo.

That did not mean another hegemonic war was inevitable. Nuclear weapons, economic interdependence, global ecological problems had altered the calculus of conflict and cooperation. But wars had certainly not disappeared, states become less selfish, standards of living more equal. The central problem of international relations, as Carr had written, was how to achieve peaceful change in an established order run by those who had created and benefitted from it. The dynamic of differential growth ruled out stability, however relatively stable the bipolar world of the Cold War might seem. Prolonged economic stagnation could threaten the USSR as much as, indeed even more acutely than, the USA. Uneven development would not spare communism either. Was China waiting in the wings?

Keohane and his colleagues continued unperturbed. The

following year, after a productive conclave at Palm Springs, *International Organization* celebrated a decade of research on 'International Regimes' with another bumper special issue. This time too, there was a solitary discordant voice. From London, Susan Strange observed that the notion of international regimes was an American academic fad that had emerged in response to perceptions of US decline amid the troubles of Watergate and mishaps of Carter, and now the arrival of Reagan, when in reaction to the nationalist turn in the White House, liberals asked themselves how 'the damage could be minimised' by refurbishing 'mechanisms of multilateral management— "regimes"'. Their concern was misplaced. The real America was not falling, but it was one they preferred not to see: a global empire achieved by a combination of military pacts and open markets. 'This special form of non-territorial imperialism is something that many American academics, brought up as liberals and internationalists, find it hard to recognise. US hegemony, while it is as nonterritorial as Britain's India in the days of John Company or Britain's Egypt after 1886, is still a form of imperialism. The fact that this nonterritorial empire extends more widely today and is even more tolerant of the pretensions of petty principalities than Britain was of those of the maharajahs merely means that it is larger and more secure. It is not much affected by temporary shocks or setbacks'. International institutions were in the first instance strategic instruments of US will, if also usefully adaptive to allied objectives, and helpfully symbolic of yearnings for a better world to which governments pay homage and no attention. America, like its rival, continued to escalate its accumulation of weapons and intervene militarily in its zones of control. The dollar continued to dominate international finance, and deregulation of markets was the work not of private agents but of the American state. Recent changes still left 'the United States undisputed hegemon of the system'.[8]

A decade later, the US had won the Cold War. Fears of decline dissipated, the anxious terms of the seventies were no longer in order. Keohane's partner Nye, the more politically ambitious of the two, had risen to advisory work for the National Security Council under Carter, and now, on the eve of the Clinton Administration where he would become Assistant Secretary at the Pentagon, could write their epitaph. *Bound to Lead* (1991) was a manifesto for the new epoch. Hegemony was a confused and unwelcome concept, which should be retired. The United States had never been a hegemon, let alone an empire. The *pax Americana*, like the *pax Britannica* before it, was a historical myth. What the United States enjoyed was 'soft power'. Cooptive rather than coercive, it was just as important as the hard power of command. 'If a state can make its power legitimate in the eyes of others, it will encounter less resistance to its wishes. If its culture and ideology are attractive, others will more willingly follow. If it can establish international norms that are consistent with its society, it will be less likely to have to change. If it can help support institutions that encourage other states to channel or limit their activities in ways the dominant state prefers, it may not need to make many costly exercises of coercive or hard power.'[9] Happily, along with its other, firmer means of enforcing its will, no country in the world was so blessed with such soft power as the United States. Richly endowed with both, it was uniquely equipped to rise to the challenges of transnational interdependence. Americans needed to overcome their

---

8 'Cave! Hic Dragones: A Critique of Regime Analysis', *International Organization*, Spring 1982, pp. 481–4.

9 *Bound to Lead: The Changing Nature of American Power*, New York 1991, pp. 19, 108, 65, 31–2.

complacency and parochialism. Before them lay a responsibility that only they could fulfill, leadership of a world in sore need of it.

7

FADE-OUT

The American exchanges of the seventies over hegemonic stability and regime theory developed in a *vase close*, unaware of what by that time was a world-wide diffusion of the legacy of Gramsci.[1] In Italy, this had traced an arc fundamentally determined by the political evolution of the PCI which he had once led. His notebooks, transferred after his death by Tatiana Schucht to Moscow, were brought back to Italy by Togliatti, who had succeeded him as leader of the party and could see the enormous intellectual asset they offered it. Capitalising on them, however, involved two difficulties. In prison, Gramsci had expressed views of other revolutionary leaders of Lenin's generation—Luxemburg, Trotsky, Bordiga—still taboo in the Stalinized Communist movement of the Cold War period. There was also the problem that Gramsci, a few days before his arrest in 1926, had sharply dissented from Stalin's repression of the Left Opposition in Russia, in a letter to Togliatti in Moscow, and as his fellow communists in prison with him subsequently explained to the party's command in

---

1   Introducing his pet coinage a decade later, Nye referred second-hand to Gramsci, of whom there is no sign he had ever read a line, any more than Keohane of Kautsky, whose idea of ultra-imperialism makes a brief appearance in *After Hegemony*.

exile, rejected the sectarian line of the Comintern in the early thirties. These awkward realities had to be concealed, in a time when party leaders told militants that they could not understand Gramsci properly without the help of Stalin and Zhdanov. The first publication of his notebooks, which came between 1948 and 1951, was accordingly an expurgated version. Rightly presented as a patrimony for all Italians, the richness of their explorations of the country's social, political and cultural history, and the nobility of Gramsci's letters from prison (a much more expurgated edition of which had appeared earlier), won the PCI an exceptional prestige, attracting a great many of the best Italian intellectuals of the time to it, and giving it a national standing no other Western Communist party ever enjoyed.

Prestige was one thing; purposive use was another. Gramsci's thought, though set down in discontinuous notes, had aimed to an extent unlike that of any previous Marxist at a unitary synthesis of history and strategy, covering at once the legacy of the pre-capitalist past, the pattern of the capitalist present and the objective of a socialist future in his country. For the PCI what mattered were the strategic implications that could be drawn from what he had left. Togliatti had returned to Italy in 1944 declaring that the anti-fascist task of the party was to build democracy, not socialism, and sought a coalition with Christian Democracy—confirming the Lateran Pact with the Vatican—to do so. Ejected from government by the DC in 1947, and heavily defeated at the polls in 1948, during the high Cold War the PCI made no great case of the place of hegemony in Gramsci's thought. The party continued along its moderate path in Italy, while keeping faith with the Soviet Union abroad, and its doctrinal orthodoxy. When crisis came with the Hungarian Revolt in 1956, Antonio Giolitti, the party's most distinguished dissident, based his reasoned exit from it on the originality of

Gramsci's conception of hegemony, arguing that this outlined a path to power in the West free of violence, based on the productive force of the working-class and the democratic institutions of a parliamentary state. 'The concept of the hegemony of the proletariat is not a synonym or variant of the concept of the dictatorship of the proletariat.'[2] In reply, Togliatti's deputy and successor Longo told him firmly that there could be no question of counterposing the hegemony to the dictatorship of the proletariat, which were complementary objectives.[3]

By the sixties, this posture had become untenable. The Twenty-Second Congress of the CPSU, going further than the Twentieth in destalinization, weakened obligations to Moscow. At home the PSI, which had been a mass party too after the war, ended its alliance with the PCI, entering government with the DC; while not long afterwards a new generation of workers, students and intellectuals exploded in a social rebellion to the left of the party. Both offered their own interpretations of Gramsci, at variance with what had hitherto been his official canonisation by the PCI. In these new conditions, the party would come to reverse its position, deciding that Gramsci had not after all been a Leninist. The hegemony of the working class

---

2 *Riforme e rivoluzione*, Turin 1957, pp. 24–6, 29–37 ff. Grandson of the ruler against whom Gramsci had fought in 1920–1921, Giolitti joined the PCI under fascism and led one of the most effective partisan groups against the Axis in the Second World War. After joining the PSI in 1957 and serving in Centre-Left governments of the sixties, he broke with Craxi in the eighties, and ended his career as an independent senator elected on a PCI list.

3 Luigi Longo, *Revisionismo nuovo e antico*, Turin 1957: 'The concept of the hegemony of the proletariat defines the internal relations of the forces of renewal and revolution; the concept of dictatorship defines the external relations of these forces with those of conservatism and counter-revolution. Far from excluding or opposing each other, the two diverse concepts are inter-connected, indeed complement each other': pp. 36–45. After hearing Giolitti out at the Eighth Party Congress before his departure, Togliatti commented curtly: 'Let's not joke about Gramsci'.

he had envisaged, its theorists now explained, was a peaceful democratic process, the fruit of a gradual cultural ascendancy in civil society, and the achievement of an electoral majority in parliament. Eurocommunism, as it could now be called, would be purely consensual, unmarred by any hint of coercion. Aiming to bypass the Socialist Party, and dispatch the assorted insurgencies to its left, the party announced the goal of a 'Historic Compromise' with Christian Democracy to advance Italian democracy, lending its support to the Andreotti governments of the mid-seventies.

Nothing came of this project, other than a steady decline in its vote.[4] PSI intellectuals, well aware of the tactical intention of the PCI, unleashed a sharp attack on its manipulation of the image of Gramsci, pointing out his unaltered Leninist convictions. Within another decade, further reduced, the party had moved yet again, this time—its thinkers declared—beyond Gramsci, who was now returned full circle to his starting place, with the signs reversed: for it had to be admitted Gramsci had indeed been the product of a totalitarian culture, which no longer had any place in the politics of the PCI. With the dissolution of the party in the nineties, his name disappeared as any official reference in its successor formations, each more loyal to the order of capital than the last. The Istituto Gramsci survives, its director explaining that Gramsci's central hope, in notebooks mercifully free of talk of imperialism, was that 'the interdependence of the world economy would be restored under the impulsion of the

---

4   For critical observations on the way party intellectuals had lowered Gramsci's conception of hegemony to the political requirements of the moment, see Guido Liguori, *Gramsci conteso*, Rome 1996, pp. 196–7, a generally honourable history of Gramsci's reception in Italy in the half century after the War, from the standpoint of a loyal member of the PCI saddened by its end, which he later recounted in *La Morte del PCI*, Rome 2009. Liguori would publish an expanded and updated version of his book in 2012.

United States'—all roads leading to Washington.[5] For another prominent collaborator with the Institute, Gramsci had clearly broken with communism and become a liberal democrat in prison.[6]

That such could be the epilogue to the reception of Gramsci in his native land is a commentary on the uses to which his ideas were put by the PCI. Formally, strategy was in command. But his conceptions were so repeatedly instrumentalised in the service of changing objectives that they became not strategy but ideology, malleable adornments of whatever line the party was taking in a given period. A great mass party was built around Gramsci's fame, no small achievement, and an enormous literature accreted around what he had written in jail—by the late eighties, some 4,000 titles. But when the party was wound up, it had little to show for its twists and turns, and the literature was far more commentary than creative application. Gramsci's conception of strategy certainly hinged on his notion of hegemony, but this was embedded in a range of interconnected concepts—war of position/war of manoeuvre, organic crisis, parliamentarism, passive revolution, subaltern classes, a taxonomy of intellectuals and more—that he devised as heuristic tools for an exploration of Italian society covering rulers and ruled, economy and class, religion and philosophy, city and country, education

5   Giuseppe Vacca, *Vita e pensieri di Antonio Gramsci*, Turin 2012, p. 149, unwittingly reproducing Keohane and Nye virtually word for word. Worldwide leadership towards a more planned economy would come from 'the most modern of bourgeoisies' in America, not from a primitive Russia with its crude methods under Stalin, and under US guidance the communist movement could play a valuable 'subaltern' role in this evolution, as a 'supporting actor' (*comprimario*): p. 140.
6   Franco Lo Piparo, *I due carceri di Gramsci*, Bari 2012, where Gramsci becomes 'the Trojan horse of liberalism' in the communist movement, from which Mussolini protected him in prison, pp. 116, 123—a work gaining the widest publicity and a high-profile literary prize.

and literature, folklore and art. His example was not followed. Gramsci began with reflections on the hegemony of Cavour and the Moderates in the nineteenth century, and had much to say about Fordism in the twentieth. In all its time, not a single serious work on Christian Democracy was ever produced by the PCI, nor a sociological study of the transformations of the Italian workforce and industry that caught it by surprise in the sixties. Empirical curiosity went by the board. [7]

Since the PCI was never coextensive with the Italian left, which contained other significant currents, not a few sharply at variance with it, the legacy of Gramsci could never be completely monopolised by the party, and in the sixties and seventies, alongside wholesale rejection of it as the ideology of a compromised formation, there emerged an alternative reading of it, centred on the key role of factory councils in his early *Ordine Nuovo* writings, counterposing the idea of workers' autonomy in these to the elevation of the party as a 'modern prince' in the *Notebooks*. Though often spirited enough in expression, this was a reaction-formation that could not dislodge the undulating sequence of established recensions based on the prison writings. The net result, as both PCI and these thorns in its side eventually faded away, was a sterilisation of Gramsci's legacy in his homeland.

Creative employment, free from institutional constraints, migrated abroad. There is inevitably something arbitrary in illustrating the result. But among possible candidates, there

---

7 Failings noted by Donald Sassoon, whose *Togliatti e la Via Italiana al Socialismo. Il PCI dal 1944 al 1964* (Turin 1980), written in a spirit of overall if not uncritical admiration, was obliged to conclude its assessment of the upshot of the party's strategy on a skeptical note, observing the danger that the PCI could suffer the defeat of obtaining the legitimation it had sought for so long 'at the price of becoming what used to be called "the alternative party of the bourgeoisie" ': p. 378.

can be no doubt of four leading—arguably the four leading—appropriations of Gramsci's thought since the eighties, viewed comparatively. Do they form a pattern? Strikingly, in certain respects. All came from thinkers far from their homelands. All emerged within the Anglosphere—the UK, US, Australia—within less than a decade of each other, between the mid-eighties and mid-nineties. All were highly individual constructions, yet each was also the fruit of a common project. All were centred around Gramsci's concept of hegemony.

8

SEQUELS

Britain was the first case where naturalisation of Gramsci produced what his domestication in Italy had not: substantive original analysis of the social and political topography of the country, setting new markers for an understanding of what might become of it. In the UK reception of Gramsci went back to the early sixties, when he was still scarcely known outside Italy.[1] A decade later, the starting-point for the major influence of his writing came with an essay by Raymond Williams, in which he at once endorsed and developed Gramsci's conception of hegemony as a 'central system of practices, meanings and values saturating the consciousness of a society at a much deeper level than ordinary notions of ideology'. Emphasising that any such hegemony always involved a complex set of structures that had to be continually 'renewed, recreated and defended', actively adjusting to and where possible incorporating alternative practices and meanings, Williams distinguished two types of oppositional culture, each traceable to a class, capable of escaping such incorporation: residual and emergent—that is, rooted

---

1   For particulars, see David Forgacs, 'Gramsci and Marxism in Britain', *New Left Review* I/176, July–August 1989, pp. 74–7.

either in a past or in what might prove a future. There were also other, less assignable practices and values that characteristically eluded hegemonic capture. For by definition, Williams insisted, hegemony was selective: 'no mode of production, and therefore no dominant society or order of society, and therefore no dominant culture, in reality exhausts human practice, human energy, human intention'.[2]

These axioms could be taken as prompts for the achievement of Stuart Hall, who arrived from Jamaica to study English literature at Oxford in the early fifties. A founder of *Universities and Left Review* in 1957 and editor of *New Left Review* in 1960, by 1964 he had joined the Centre for Contemporary Cultural Studies in Birmingham, whose collaborative work he would come to direct for a decade. There he began from the mid-seventies onwards to analyse sea changes in British politics, and with striking accuracy to predict their outcomes, in what remains the most clairvoyant single example of a Gramscian diagnostic of a given society on record.[3] A year into the Labour government elected in 1974, in a collection entitled *Resistance through Rituals*, he co-authored an analysis of subcultures in—principally, but not exclusively—working-class youth, as an area of latent recalcitrance within a dominant culture whose hegemony was never either stably homeostatic or wholly absorptive, forming at best a mobile equilibrium that had continually to be recast to control practices at variance with

---

2   'Base and Superstructure in Marxist Theory', *New Left Review* I/82, November–December 1973, pp. 8–13: arguments expanded in Williams's subsequent account of hegemony in *Marxism and Literature*, Oxford 1977, pp. 108–27.

3   For the assurance of Hall's command of Gramsci's problematics, see from a later period, 'Gramsci's Relevance for the Study of Race and Ethnicity', *Journal of Communication Inquiry*, June 1986, pp. 5–27. Althusser and Poulantzas were other influences: for the latter, 'Nicos Poulantzas: 'State, Power, Socialism', *New Left Review* I/119, January–February 1980, pp. 60–9.

it.[4] Three years later, another collective work, *Policing the Crisis*, focussed on successive moral panics—at threatening spectres of youth revolt, black immigration, trade-union militancy—in a time of sharp economic crisis and social turbulence, which were triggering a social backlash of petty-bourgeois stamp. Mounting demands for the reimposition of social discipline were already reflected in the shift from Heath to Thatcher in the Conservative opposition. Labour, after first trying merely to 'manage dissensus', was now drifting with this mood towards greater repression, in a swing of the pendulum towards a condition in which 'coercion becomes, as it were, the natural and routine form in which consent is secured'. That did not mean Britain faced any violent crackdown from above, along Chilean lines. Rather, while all the forms of a post-liberal state remained intact, a tougher government posture could rely on 'a powerful ground-swell of popular legitimacy'.[5] Looming was an authoritarian populism.

Writing a month before Thatcher came to power in 1979, Hall warned that social democracy had shown itself incapable of mastering what had become an organic crisis of the post-war settlement, to which Thatcherism was now offering a potent response. Weaving together contradictory strands of monetarist neoliberalism and organicist Toryism, it was seeking to construct a new common sense, as Gramsci understood this. Identifying freedom with the market and order with moral tradition, it was binding together the opportunities of the one with the values of the other in a single package for popular consumption. This was a hegemonic project, whose attractive

4 Stuart Hall and Tony Jefferson (eds), *Resistance through Rituals: Youth Sub-Cultures in Post-War Britain*, London 1975, pp. 38–42 ff.

5 Stuart Hall, Chas Critcher, Tony Jefferson, John Clarke and Brian Roberts, *Policing the Crisis*, pp. 307–16.

effects could already be seen in the public debate over failures of schooling under Callaghan.[6]

Once Thatcher was in power, Hall developed these propositions across the next decade, correctly predicting her second and third electoral victories. The left had suffered a lasting defeat in Britain, as it had in Italy in the twenties: Gramsci's stock of concepts bore directly on local experience. While it was true that Thatcher never commanded a numerical majority of the electorate, and her ascendancy was always contested by much of the population, she had welded together a range of social agents, reaching from bankers and professionals through small employers to skilled workers, that formed a historic bloc in his sense. Intuitively, Thatcherism had understood that social interests are often contradictory, that ideologies need not be coherent, that identities are seldom stable, and had worked on all three to form new popular subjects embodying its hegemony. That hegemony, as Gramsci had laid down, necessarily had an economic nucleus: financial deregulation and privatisation of utilities for the City, lower taxes for the middle class, wage growth for skilled workers, sale of council houses for the masses at large. But encapsulating all of these was Thatcher's version of a Gramscian 'passive revolution': the ideological promise of an overdue modernity, in a country which had never known the second round of capitalist transformation that had reinvigorated post-war Germany or Japan. The key to her success lay in the paradox of a 'regressive modernisation'.[7]

This was a compelling analysis of Thatcher's regime, by any measure. Missing, certainly, was any international framework, as Reagan consolidated his—more widely based—rule in the

---

6   'The Great Moving Right Show', in *The Hard Road to Renewal*, London 1988, pp. 39–56.

7   'Gramsci and Us', *The Hard Road to Renewal*, pp. 162, 164, 167.

United States, and neoliberal recipes spread across the advanced capitalist world. But no political reading of a conjuncture is ever exhaustive, and Hall's was construed to serve a purpose: the best way to resist and remove the Conservative regime in Britain. That must involve meeting it on its own ground, he argued, with the vision of another kind of modernity, offering a more generous and radical emancipation from the past. That would have to be fought out across the whole space of civil society, as well as over the state, and could not afford to lapse into postures of indifference or disdain towards areas and issues traditionally regarded as less than political—gender, race, family, sexuality, education, consumption, leisure, nature—as well as work, wages, taxes, health, or communications. The small end of the market had to be respected, where an artisanal capitalism offered a zone of variety and choice, and the left ought never to let itself be 'cut off from the landscape of popular pleasures'. But its aim should be to match the ambitions of its adversary: not to reform but transform society.

In Italy, a mass party that inherited the ideas of Gramsci sterilised them, producing little original analysis of the society surrounding it, and no coherent strategy for changing it. In Britain, it was the reverse: an original analysis was produced, and elements of a strategy consistent with it proposed, but there was no vehicle for executing it. Hall's interventions were published in the journal of the small Communist Party of Great Britain that followed the PCI into Eurocommunism and self-extinction. That left the Labour Party, where Hall had a less certain touch. Criticising its narrow-minded statism and instinctive hostility to democratic participation, let alone mobilisation, he nevertheless more or less explicitly approved, in the name of a relative modernisation, the determination of the party's leadership to purge it of a left regarded as even more backward, and while not without misgivings, initially garlanded Blair with laudatory epithets,[8] before concluding that New Labour—its every second word 'modern'—was a let-down, extending rather than displacing the overall parameters of Thatcherism. The much deeper grasp of the nature of the party to be found in the first reception of Gramsci in the UK, in the work of Tom Nairn, would have saved him his disappointment.[9]

It was Nairn, too, who saw the other side of the conjuncture that triggered Hall's project, which remained an absence in it throughout. For Gramsci in Italy, a critical component of any full hegemony was the creation of a 'national-popular' will and culture. In Hall's reception, the popular moment effaces, all but completely, the national. The strains which Thatcher was putting on 'Ukanian' unity, already beginning to fray when Nairn published *The Break-Up of Britain* (1977), in the same years Hall was developing his account of the break-up of the post-war political settlement, he scarcely noticed. There was perhaps a reason for that. Britain, as Nairn explained, was not and never had been a nation: it was a composite kingdom of the early modern period, which had survived beyond its time as the greatness of an empire. But what Thatcherism trumpeted as a still-imperial identity—bodied forth by British aircraft carriers in the South Atlantic seas—was starting to become a multi-cultural *pis-aller*

---

8   From 'a remarkable show of political courage', to 'genuine humanity': see 'Parties on the Verge of a Nervous Breakdown', *Soundings* No 1, Autumn 1995, pp. 23, 26; 'The Great Moving Nowhere Show', *Marxism Today*, revenant issue, November–December 1998, p. 14, where despite many otherwise sharp criticisms, New Labour still had 'a substantial claim on our support'.

9   Tom Nairn, 'The Nature of the Labour Party', *New Left Review* I/27, September–October 1964, pp. 38–65, and I/28, November–December 1964, pp. 3–62; 'Labour Imperialism', I/32, July–August 1965, pp. 3–15 ; see also 'The English Working Class', I/24, March–April 1964, pp. 43–57, and 'Hugh Gaitskell', I/25, May–June 1964, pp. 63–8.

for immigrants from the empire, less impassible than English, if inevitably subordinate to the historic valences of Great Britain. It is little wonder that a Jamaican conscious of the fate, not just of his own island but of the Caribbean as a whole, would turn away from this inextricable knot around the throat of the national, as Gramsci conceived it.[10]

So too the very reassertion of the nation's position in the world that was Thatcher's proudest boast, as the British example to all peoples in putting freedom first, was eventually her undoing, as the European integration she had helped accelerate closed around her like a trap, a subtler Italian ruler bringing her down in a way that had no place in Hall's account of her hold on power. Did that upshot cast a retrospective light on fault lines within his construction of hegemony under Thatcherism? In some measure, undeniably. The two-fold torsion twisting Ukania—caught between Edinburgh and Brussels—out of

10 'I'm not and never will be "English"', he would say in his most personal account of the family background in Jamaica from which he came, and his experience of the imperial society in which he arrived: interview in David Morley and Kuan-Hsing Chen (eds), *Stuart Hall: Critical Dialogues in Cultural Studies*, London-New York 1996, p. 490; see too his lecture 'Negotiating Caribbean Identities', *New Left Review* I/209, January–February 1995, pp. 3–14. His contribution to the History Workshop volume edited by Raphael Samuel in 1981, *People's History and Socialist Theory*—'Notes on Deconstructing the "Popular"'—cites Gramsci on the national-popular, but confines itself to the second half of the hyphenation. Samuel, by contrast, went on to edit three volumes devoted to *Patriotism: The Making and Unmaking of British National Identity* (1989), in which he explained self-critically that the History Workshop had 'played some small part in the recrudescence of cultural nationalism', trying indeed to 'expel foreign words from our pages'. But now it was plumping for 'British' over 'English' as more hospitable to newcomers and outsiders, while keeping 'Gramscian notions of hegemony' firmly at bay as elitist (anticipating later objections to these by James Scott). The relationship between Hall and Samuel, the two central figures of the early New Left, would make a fascinating study. The finest piece of writing Hall ever composed was his tribute to his dead friend: 'Raphael Samuel: 1934–1999', *New Left Review* I/221, January–February 1997, pp. 119–27.

shape today was already visible then. Correlatively, although
he had emphasised a gathering swing towards coercion in the
seventies, his writing in the eighties underplayed its part in
securing Thatcher's grip on the country, when the two decisive
victories that gave her supremacy, after an uncertain start, were
both exercises in violence: the crushing of the miners strike, and
the colonial war for the Falklands. Neither received commen-
surate emphasis. When New Labour came to power there was
a similar blind spot. Dubbing Blair's regime 'The Great Moving
Nowhere Show' was ill-advised: it would soon be moving,
guns in hand, to Pristina and Basra. Conversely, in the consent
Thatcher achieved, the accent fell too persistently on ideological
capture at the expense of material inducements, and ideological
motifs themselves became—never explicitly, but with insuf-
ficient precaution—too liable to disconnexion from any social
anchorage, as if they could float free in any political direction
at the wand of an adept enough conjuror. Hall could and would
never have taken this step. But the door was left ajar for it.

II

There, a parallel enterprise had left traces in its approach. At
the end of the sixties, some two decades after Hall arrived from
Jamaica, an immigrant close to him in age arrived in Britain
from Argentina. Ernesto Laclau, trained in history in Buenos
Aires, had been a militant in the small National Party of the
Independent Left, founded by Jorge Abelardo Ramos, virtually
the only socialist thinker of his generation to argue for support of
Perón from the outset of his rule in the forties.[11] On disembarking
for Oxford, Laclau's first publication in English was a classical

11   See Laclau's own remarks in *New Reflections on the Revolution of Our Time*,
London-New York, 1990, pp. 197–201.

Marxist analysis of the social constellation in Argentina that
had produced the Onganía dictatorship, and the great political
uprising of the Cordobazo against it in May 1969.[12] After moving
from the discipline of history to government in securing a position at Essex, he produced a collection of four essays, *Politics and
Ideology in Marxist Theory*, making a notably original, if always
critical use of Althusserian concepts, which had a major impact
on Hall's thinking about Thatcherism.[13]

By this time, Laclau was already working closely with another
immigrant, Chantal Mouffe, a Belgian whose training was in
philosophy, which she had been teaching in Colombia. Together
in 1985, they published *Hegemony and Socialist Strategy*, bringing post-structuralism boldly to bear on the Marxist tradition,
in political sympathy with what had been Eurocommunism,
but in theoretical outlook now declaratively post-Marxist.
Reviewing the history of the Second and Third Internationals,
they concluded that both had remained trapped in the illusion
that ideologies corresponded to classes, and historical development led by economic necessity to the triumph of socialism.
What neither had been able to resolve was the existence, not
only of divisions within the working class as the carrier of this
supposed necessity in the shape of the revolutionary subject
of history, but also of non-capitalist classes that did not form
part of the working class. The problems these posed had met
only incoherent responses, successively from Plekhanov and
Labriola, Bernstein and Kautsky, Luxemburg and Trotsky. A
first, if still quite narrow, move beyond their failures came with

12 'Argentina—Imperialist Strategy and the May Crisis', leading article, *New Left Review* I/62, July–August 1970, pp. 3–21.
13 *Politics and Ideology in Marxist Theory: Capitalism—Fascism—Populism*, London-New York 1977. Hall was more reserved about Laclau's later work: see 'On Postmodernism and Articulation. An interview with Stuart Hall', in *Stuart Hall: Critical Dialogues in Cultural Studies*, pp. 146–7.

Lenin's notion of the hegemony of the proletariat, which involved some articulation of proletarian objectives with demands of the peasantry. But it was Gramsci who made the real breakthrough, by deepening Lenin's conception in two ways: transforming the idea of hegemony from a merely political to a moral and intellectual form of leadership, and understanding that the subject of a hegemony could not be any socio-economically pre-constituted class, but had to be a politically constructed collective will—a force capable of synthesising heteroclite demands that had no necessary connexion with each other, and could take sharply different directions, into a national-popular unity.

This, Laclau and Mouffe observed, was a signal advance. But Gramsci had still retained the idea that the proletariat was structurally a 'fundamental class', and in thinking that a consensual 'war of position' could be combined with a coercive 'war of movement' in the West, had failed to break cleanly with Bolshevism. The way forward was now to scrap all residues of class essentialism and drop any idea of a war of movement. Rather than interests giving rise to ideologies, discourses created subject-positions, and the goal today should not be socialism but a 'radical democracy', of which socialism would—since capitalism bred relations of undemocratic subordination—remain a dimension, not the other way round.[14] In Laclau's subsequent work, *On Populist Reason*, reference to socialism fades altogether, and populism takes over hegemony as the more pointed and powerful signifier of the inherently contingent unification of democratic demands—which in isolation could equally well be woven into an anti-democratic discourse—into a collective will. Bound together by a common set of symbols and affective ties to a leader, an insurgent people can then confront the

---

14 *Hegemony and Socialist Strategy*, London-New York 1985, p. 178.

regnant powers of their society, across the dividing line of a dichotomous antagonism between the two.

First proposed in the time of Thatcher and Reagan, this was a formal schema that anticipated developments in Europe thirty years later, when deindustrialisation had shrunk and divided the working class, leaving a much more fragmented social landscape and a multiplication of movements, of right and left, contesting the established order in the name of the people—'populism' becoming the bugbear of elites across the EU.[15] Hall had foreseen the rise of Thatcherism in the eighties. No less impressively, Laclau and Mouffe were augurs of the reaction against neoliberalism post-2008. In these conditions, Laclau and Mouffe realised what Hall could not: the adoption of their vision by a political force with mass support. In Spain, the leaders of Podemos—they too with a season in Latin America behind them—based its strategy expressly on their prescriptions for a hegemonic populism.[16] By any standards, this was no small achievement for a theoretical system of often forbidding

---

15 For which, see Marco D'Eramo's scathing reconstruction of the history behind current diatribes: 'Populism and the New Oligarchy', *New Left Review* II/82 July–August 2013, pp. 5–28; and for a spirited recent vindication of the term by Chantal Mouffe, 'El Momento Populista', *El País*, 10 June 2016. In what follows, there is injustice to Mouffe, whose writing—in particular its engagement with Schmitt, with a resolve to render antagonistic into agonistic contradictions within a democratic political system—forms a distinct body of work, alongside that co-authored with Laclau.

16 See the dialogue between Íñigo Errejón and Chantal Mouffe, *Construir Pueblo. Hegemonía y radicalización de la democracia*, Madrid 2015, passim. Both authors explain that their real political awakening came in Latin America—Colombia for Mouffe, Bolivia for Errejón, pp. 72–3. In Argentina too, Laclau was not a prophet without honour in his own country, ending his days esteemed by Cristina Fernández Kirchner, and in vigorous support of her. See the indignant conservative profile, 'Ernesto Laclau, el Ideólogo de la Argentina Dividida' in *Noticias de la Semana*, 13 April, and the lively and affectionate tribute by Robin Blackburn, 'Ernesto Laclau 1935–2014', 14 April 2014, versobooks.com

technicality. But political efficacy is one thing and intellectual cogency another. The aporias in this case were evident.

The linguistic turn of the theory, in common with its late-twentieth-century vogue in general, proposes a discursive idealism severing significations from any stable connexion with referents. Here the result has been to detach ideas and demands so completely from socio-economic moorings that they can in principle be appropriated by any agency for any political construct. Inherently, the range of articulations knows no limit. All is contingency: expropriation of the expropriators could become the watchword of bankers, secularisation of church lands a goal of the Vatican, destruction of guilds the ideal of craftsmen, mass redundancies the call of a working class, enclosures the aim of a peasantry. The proposal defeats itself. Not only can anything be articulated in any direction: everything becomes articulation. First hegemony, then populism, are presented as a type of politics, among others. Then, in a characteristic inflationary move, they become the definition of all politics as such—thereby making themselves supernumerary.[17]

If extravagances of this kind can be set aside as gestures to fashion, other features of the construction are more significant. Hegemony, as in the PCI tradition, is advanced as a strategy without a topography. Though the national-popular is taken as a key objective, it is unaccompanied by any description of a national scenery. The contrast with Laclau's analysis of Peronism in Argentina before he reached post-Marxism, exemplary in

---

17 Thus: (i) At first, 'hegemony is a political *type of relation*, a *form*, if one so wishes, of politics'; then it becomes 'the field of the political' as such—a game that has 'a name: hegemony': *Hegemony and Socialist Strategy*, pp. 139. (ii) At first, 'populism is, quite simply, a way of constructing the political'; then 'populist reason amounts to political reason *tout court*'—indeed, is not populism 'the very condition of political action?': *On Populist Reason*, London-New York 2004, pp. 19, 225.

its penetration and detail, is striking.[18] No doubt expatriation in part accounted for the change, which in turn allowed a deracinated strategy to travel so well. But there was a conceptual logic at work too. Once hegemony went automatically populist, there was no call for any precision in characterising the social chequerboard. 'The language of a populist discourse—whether of Right or Left is always going to be imprecise and fluctuating', Laclau remarked, but this 'vagueness and imprecision' was not a cognitive failure, since social reality itself was so heterogeneous and volatile.[19] No need—or indeed possibility?—therefore of the kind of fine-grained analysis that Marx supplied of France, Lenin of Russia, Mao of China, Gramsci of Italy. Lauding the Occupy slogan of '99 versus 1 percent', Mouffe's interlocutor in Spain explains that a hegemonic discourse is 'not statistical but performative'.[20] For such a performance, particulars can be an impediment, vagueness a virtue—the condition of political effect.

Vaguest, for populist reason, is necessarily delineation of the adversary, since to specify it too accurately or realistically risks casting the net of hegemonic interpellations too narrowly, exposing the rhetorical percentages as the fiction they are. Errejón prudently declines to unpack *la casta* against which Podemos summons *la gente* to rise in his own country.[21] The

---

18 *Politics and Ideology in Marxist Theory*, London 1977, pp. 176–91, where 'the massive presence of the working-class in Peronism gave it an exceptional ability to persist as a movement', and political discourse had a 'double articulation', to ideas of the people and to structural positions in relations of production: pp. 190, 194.

19 *On Populist Reason*, p. 118.

20 *Construir Pueblo*, p. 105; for use of the same contrast and conception of 'performative', pp. 118, 121.

21 Mouffe expresses some skepticism at the debonair usage of the latter, whose Anglophone equivalent would be Obama's fondness for 'folks', as memorably in his breezy aside on his country's security services: 'we tortured some folks'. Defending his use of *la casta*, Errejón remarks

political motives for such reticence are intelligible. Its theoretical counterpart, however, is a void. Where Gramsci began his reflections on hegemony with an analysis of the ruling bloc in the Risorgimento, in Laclau and Mouffe's construction those above have all but vanished into the thinnest of abstractions, becoming simply the 'institutions' or the 'institutional system', never further specified, as if to give any face to the forces arrayed against those below could only weaken morale. So logically, notwithstanding formal clauses to the contrary, hegemony becomes in practice a matter for the ruled alone—as in: 'there is no hegemony without constructing popular identity out of a plurality of democratic demands'.[22] Gramsci would have been astonished. What opposes such hegemonic unification is 'institutional differentiation'—a shadowy divide and rule that remains anonymous.[23] The historically normal forms of hegemony, which have always been those of the dominant classes, are dispatched offstage.

It follows that there is no balance sheet of the political experiences that *On Populist Reason* offers as illustrations of its case, which would involve consideration not just of the construction of new subject-positions from below, but of the objective conditions for such a 'populist rupture', conceded to be necessary for it to appear, and the objective upshots of its trajectory, in late nineteenth century United States or twentieth century Argentina, or anywhere else. Symptomatically, all that could be said of the fate of American Populism in the 1890s were three terse words: 'institutional differentiations prevailed'.[24] In this account,

---

that 'its mobilising power lies in its indefinition': *Construir Pueblo*, pp. 121–2.

22 *On Populist Reason*, p. 95

23 Or, more rarely 'institutional totalisation', denying any outside to the community: *On Populist Reason*, pp. 80–1.

24 *On Populist Reason*, p. 208.

Togliatti, Tito and Mao were commendably national-populist, if
hampered by the retrograde internationalism of the Comintern;
why one should have failed, and the others not, exceeds the
brief. Where interpellations are all, definitions have little weight.
Podemos can reject social democracy one day, declare itself the
new social democracy the next.[25] Teething problems, perhaps.
But a long way from the prisoner of Bari.

III

Gramsci's afterlife took a sharply different turn in Asia. In 1947, a
young Bengali militant of the Communist Party of India arrived
in Paris to work as a cadre in the World Federation of Democratic
Youth, set up by the Soviet Union as the Cold War broke over
Europe. Ranajit Guha was then twenty-five. After spending the
next six years travelling like a Comintern emissary of old in the
Middle East, North Africa, Europe East and West, the USSR
and China, he returned to Bengal, working first in the mills and
docks, then teaching and researching history in local colleges.
In 1956 he resigned from the party over the Soviet invasion in
Hungary, and three years later moved to England, lecturing for
two decades at Manchester and Sussex. In 1970–1971, a sabbati-
cal in India coincided with the savage repression of the Naxalite
peasant insurgency in Bengal, in which both branches of Indian
Communism—split since 1964 between pro-Russian and pro-
Chinese wings—colluded.[26] Resolving to work henceforward

---

25 Pablo Iglesias, Speech at the Ritz Hotel in Madrid, 5 June 2016. Three weeks
    later, voters were incredulous. Ironically, Errejón had declined Mouffe's
    description of Podemos as populist, on the grounds that the term was
    toxic in the media—perhaps the reason why the party preferred at the
    last minute to don the reassuring *tricornio* of González and his progeny,
    to so little avail.

26 For this trajectory, see Partha Chatterjee's editorial introduction to Guha,
    The Small Voice of History: Collected Essays, Ranikhet 2009, pp. 1–17.

on peasant resistance, he convened in Sussex at the end of the decade a group of much younger Indian historians to plan a new journal, *Subaltern Studies*, whose title announced its inspiration. 'In our urge to learn from Gramsci', Guha would later write, 'we were entirely on our own and owed nothing to the mainstream communist parties', from whom the project kept its distance: 'to us, both represented a left-liberal extension of the Indian power elite itself'.[27]

In a famous opening manifesto, attacking conventional nationalist historiography of the independence movement for its restriction to elite politics, Guha called for study of the struggles of the subaltern classes—workers, peasants, non-industrial urban poor and lower sections of the petty-bourgeoisie—as an autonomous domain, in which vast swathes of popular life and consciousness escaped the official narratives of an Indian bourgeoisie, whose inability to integrate them under its leadership meant a 'historical failure of the nation to come into its own'.[28]

Across the next thirty years, *Subaltern Studies* made an indelible mark on South Asian historiography in pursuit of this programme, with original studies of popular forms of resistance in a 'history from below' more akin to the work of E. P. Thompson than to the Birmingham School. Over time, after Guha's departure from the helm at the end of the eighties, a mutation not unlike that visible in the work of Hall or Laclau set in. Under the impact of post-structuralism, there was an increasing turn to discursive constructions of power and cultural rather than material determinants of consciousness or action, though—a significant difference—reaction against

27 'Gramsci in India: Homage to a Teacher', *Journal of Modern Italian Studies*, 2011, No. 2 p. 289.
28 'On Some Aspects of the Historiography of Colonial India', *Subaltern Studies* I, Delhi 1982, pp. 1–8.

official claims of the post-independence state to modernity
and progress, rejected as an ideological patrimony of the Raj,
eventually keeled over into a sentimentalisation of peasant communities, and drift towards neo-nativism.[29]

Guha himself, a generation older and tempered in a still
undivided international communist movement, changed little.
Elementary Aspects of Peasant Insurgency in Colonial India,
which appeared—the fruit of a prior decade of work—in early
1983 within a few months of the launching of the first issue of
Subaltern Studies, united gifts whose combination is rare in any
historian: a powerful formalising theoretical mind, meticulous
empirical research, confident comparative range, not to speak
of a memorable literary *tranchant*.

The aim of *Elementary Aspects* was to demonstrate the 'sovereignty, consistency, and logic' of the conceptions and actions
of peasant rebels against landlords, moneylenders and officials
under the Raj, treated not as sequence of uprisings but as a
repertoire of forms, beginning with 'negation', and proceeding
through 'ambiguity, modality, solidarity, transmission and terri-
toriality'. On these Guha brought to bear his formidable mastery
of widely differing intellectual resources, from Propp, Vygotsky,
Lotman or Barthes on one side, through Lévi-Strauss and
Gluckman, Dumont and Bourdieu, to Hilton, Hill or Lefebvre
on the other, not to speak of Mao throughout.[30] His controlling

---

29 For a critique of this involution by one of the early editors of the journal,
    see Sumit Sarkar, 'The Decline of the Subaltern in *Subaltern Studies*', in
    Vinayak Chaturvedi, *Mapping Subaltern Studies and the Postcolonial*,
    London-New York 2000, pp. 300–23.

30 Not names dropped for mere display, as so often in subsequent literature,
    but matter-of-factly relevant to his purpose. In a foreword of graceful
    generosity—his own work is essentially antithetical—James Scott could
    write in the re-edition of *Elementary Aspects* some twenty years later: 'A
    book of great originality and large ambition might usefully be thought of
    as a shipyard. A sure mark of its influence would be how many ships were

aim was to rehabilitate Indian peasants as subjects of their own history and makers of their own rebellion. But unlike many who followed him, he was unflinching in his description of the limits to both in colonial times, refusing to ascribe a 'phoney secularism' to rebel solidarities, noting the ways in which a sense of class could be manipulated into a feeling of race, the fact that peasantry could 'produce not only rebels, but collaborators, informers, traitors', and the frequency with which armed insurgents would issue from 'single-caste settlements', inevitably a minority of villages.[31] The roseate visions of another generation were foreign to him.

So it was logical he would follow *Elementary Aspects* with a succinct masterpiece entitled *Dominance without Hegemony*, perhaps the single most striking work ever inspired by Gramsci. Its theme is the structures of power both under the Raj and in the struggle for liberation from it. In depicting these, Guha developed an analytic model of such clarity and force that he could say, without emphasis but with reason, that he hoped it might resolve ambiguities in Gramsci's writings themselves. There was, of course, a bewildering diversity of unequal relationships in colonial India. But all involved a relation of Dominance [D]

launched from its dock. By this standard alone, Ranajit Guha's *Elementary Aspects of Peasant Insurgency* has had enormous impact. Thousands of ships have since sailed forth flying his pennant. Given the fact that in this case the shipwright had more of a philosophy of boat building than a rigid design, it is not surprising that the shipyard could launch vessels of greatly varying designs, sailing to unknown ports, and carrying new and exotic cargoes. The shipwright, I imagine, would not even recognise some of these vessels as having been inspired by him and, in fact, would probably want to disown any association with quite a few. That, however, is the undeniable fate of a master-builder: his ideas are simply incorporated into the routines of shipbuilding, often without acknowledgment. Though he may often feel misrepresented and pirated, it is surely a better fate than being ignored': *Elementary Aspects of Peasant Insurgency in Colonial India*, Durham 1999, p. xi.

31 *Elementary Aspects*, pp. 173, 177, 198, 314.

to Subordination [S], each of which was constituted in turn by another pair of interacting elements—Dominance by Coercion [C] and Persuasion [P], and Subordination by Collaboration [C*] and Resistance [R], as in:

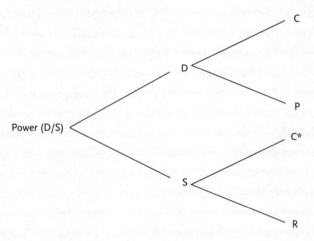

In any given society, and at any given point in time, the relation D/S varied according to what—by analogy with capital—Guha termed the 'organic composition' of power, which depended on the relative weights of C and P in D, and of C* and R in S, which were always, he argued, contingent. Hegemony was a condition of dominance in which P exceeded C—persuasion outweighing coercion. 'Defined in these terms', Guha went on, 'hegemony operates as a dynamic concept and keeps even the most persuasive structure of Dominance always and necessarily open to Resistance'. But at the same time, 'since hegemony, as we understand it, is a particular condition of D and the latter is constituted by C and P, there can be no hegemonic system under which P outweighs C to the point of reducing it to nullity. Were that to happen, there would be no Dominance, hence no hegemony'. This conception, he noted, 'avoids the Gramscian juxtaposition of domination and hegemony as antinomies', which had 'alas, provided far too often a theoretical pretext for a liberal absurdity—the absurdity of an uncoercive state—in spite of the drive of Gramsci's own work to the contrary'.[32]

Equipped with this grid, Guha proceeded to lay out the distinctive idioms at work in the four constituents of D and S under British rule. By definition, in a colonial state C prevailed over P—the Raj boasting 'one of the largest standing armies of the world, an elaborate penal system, and a highly developed police force', topped by a bureaucracy armed with emergency powers. Once British power had settled down into a 'regulated empire', the idiom of conquest gave way to an idiom of 'order', authorising not just routine repression but public health interventions, forced labour, military recruitment and more. Order did not operate in isolation, however, but interacted with an indigenous idiom complementary to it—*danda* or 'punishment', denoting all those traditional forms of power based on force and fear as manifestations of divine will in affairs of state. In the constituent P of D, on the other hand, where non-antagonistic relations were sought with the subject population, the characteristic idiom of the Raj was 'improvement'—Western-style education, patronage of Indian literary or artistic productions, Orientalist heritage projects, administrative cooption, rural paternalism, modern infrastructural works and the like. This in turn found its native complement in Hindu doctrines of *dharma*, understood as the moral duty to perform the functions allotted every human being in a caste hierarchy, an ideal perfectly adapted to modern doctrines of class conciliation, in Tagore or Gandhi.

---

32 'In short, hegemony, deduced thus from Dominance, offers us the double advantage of pre-empting a slide towards a liberal-utopian conceptualisation of the state and of representing power as a concrete historical relation informed necessarily and irreducibly by force and consent': *Dominance without Hegemony: History and Power in Colonial India*, Cambridge MA 1997, pp. 20–3.

As for S, its constituents too had their colonial and colonised versions. Collaboration was instilled both by British doctrines of 'obedience' (prominent in Gandhi before Amritsar), descending from Hume and transmitted through early Benthamism, and Indian ideologies of *bhakti*—'loyalty'—stretching back to the Bhagavad Gita. Resistance, on the other hand, could be coded in British terms as 'rightful dissent', appealing to liberal notions of natural rights dating back to Locke and expressed in (mostly) law-abiding marches, demonstrations, petitions and the like, or in local terms as 'dharmic protest'—that is, mass actions like uprisings, desertions, sit-ins, hartals, uninformed by any idea of rights, but infused with anger at the failure of rulers to perform their moral duties of protection and succour to the ruled.

The power of the Raj, resting on a massive predominance of C over P, was Dominance without Hegemony. How did matters stand in the national movement arrayed against it? Since Congress commanded no state power, to which it aspired but could not yet enjoy, and electoral representation was confined to a narrow suffrage, it was on popular mobilisation that its claim to popular consent rested. That, however, was spurious in more than one respect. Certainly, the national movement aroused genuine mass enthusiasm. But since its bourgeois leadership was incapable of integrating the class interests of workers or peasants into the movement, coercion in one form or another inevitably pervaded it from beginning to end. Destruction of goods, violent intimidation, and deployment of caste sanctions marked the early campaigns for Swadeshi. Then, in the time of Non-Cooperation, came the sanctimonious 'soul-force' of Gandhi's disciplinary system, designed to suppress any unruly or egalitarian expressions of popular feeling, castigated as 'mob-ocracy'. The elites leading the independence movement strove for hegemony, but in repressing wherever possible any hint of elemental immediacy in the struggle, could not but resort to coercive methods, and in a revenge of the repressed, in the end were unable to contain forces of communalism which, in continually denying, they were helpless to transcend.[33] In R too, P failed to prevail over C. Common to both rulers and would-be rulers in the subcontinent was a hegemonic deficit.

The power and justice of this indictment of the national movement that culminated in Partition stands. But in projecting the case forward to Congress rule of a shrunken India after independence, Guha overextended its application.[34] He saw all too clearly, and rightly insisted on, the takeover of the British apparatus of coercion lock, stock and barrel by Congress, once it was in command of the state, and its ruthless use of the same style of military and police violence to break resistance to its rule where it appeared. But he overlooked the new forms of persuasion at the disposal of the party, supplied by the post-imperial state and civil society. For now suffrage was universal, and regular elections, held on helpfully loaded British rules, could convert half or less of the country's votes into an overwhelming majority of seats in a parliament embodying a popular sovereignty unavailable under the Raj: much the most important consensual mechanism in the structure of any capitalist legitimacy. So too religion could play a less divisive role, once the party's sociology as a Hindu formation now coincided so much more closely

---

33 *Dominance without Hegemony*, pp. 131–2.

34 There is a note of uncharacteristic indecision in Guha's formulations at this point, betraying perhaps an atypical trace of nostalgia for the national movement. In *Dominance without Hegemony*, he would say 'coercion set out to compete with persuasion in the national project', without specifying the result of the competition other than negatively: p. 151. Thirty years later, he would speak of a 'leadership that had been empowered by the consent of the people in the movement for independence' which nevertheless 'failed to invest that consent into a hegemony as leaders of the new sovereign state': 'Gramsci in India', p. 294.

with the contours of the nation, caste structures holding in place electoral support across linguistic or ethnic boundaries. In these conditions, Congress entered into the inheritance of a genuine hegemony. Perhaps that conclusion, and its epilogue in today's Hindutva, was too unpalatable.

In the seventies, when he was preparing *Elementary Aspects*, Guha intervened in the political scene in India with a set of searing denunciations of torture and repression under Congress rule.[35] In the eighties, as *Subaltern Studies* got under way, he fell politically silent. Was there a connexion? Perhaps the crushing of Naxalism in Bengal extinguished in him any hope that, as far as the eye might see, the Indian masses could shake the structures of what passed for their emancipation. Unspoken may have been a conviction that no strategy, as Gramsci would have conceived it, was possible in such wilderness. Yet nothing in such a conclusion detracts from the intellectual elegance and political intransigence of *Dominance without Hegemony*.

IV

In the work of Giovanni Arrighi, born in the year that Gramsci died, two streams of thinking about hegemony that till then always had remained disjoined, as a relation of power between classes and between states, came together for the first time in a sustained synthesis. An unusual trajectory, from a management position in Unilever, through solidarity work in Rhodesia, to organisation of workers' struggles in Italy, and research on peasant migration in Calabria, gave Arrighi a unique range of experience—multinational corporation, anti-imperialist liberation, factory revolt, land and labour—for his enterprise. Out

---

35 See the five texts published between 1971 and 1979, beginning with 'On Torture and Culture', in Part V of *The Small Voice of History*, pp. 560–628.

of this came, at about the same time as Hall was working on Thatcherism, Laclau on populism, Guha on peasant insurgency, *The Geometry of Imperialism* (1977), which sought to integrate the alternative paradigms of Hobson and Lenin in a coherent set of propositions covering the sequence from British to German to American empires, and the transformations of capital accompanying them. Responding to critics in a subsequent afterword (1982), Arrighi reflected that it would have been better to designate the successive phases of imperialism he had discussed as cycles of hegemony, a theory of which his text could be read as an adumbration.[36] In the same year, his contribution to a collective volume on *Dynamics of Global Crisis*—drawing on ideas developed when he was a leader of the Gruppo Gramsci, one of the revolutionary currents in the great labour and student upsurges of the late sixties and early seventies in Italy—made it clear he had already begun to connect inter-state and intra-state planes of hegemony in a single framework.[37]

By this time, Arrighi had moved to the US and was working at SUNY Binghamton with Immanuel Wallerstein in a productive exchange of respective influences—Gramsci transmitted from the former to the latter, Braudel from the latter to the former. With *The Long Twentieth Century* (1994), whose ambition was conceived in Cosenza many years earlier, when he had dreamt of reconciling Smith and Marx, Weber and Schumpeter, he fused theory and history with a hallmark clarity of style and economy of form. For Arrighi, as for Gramsci, hegemony combined force

---

36 *The Geometry of Imperialism*, London 1983, pp. 172–3.

37 See 'A Crisis of Hegemony', in Samir Amin, Giovanni Arrighi, Andre Gunder Frank and Immanuel Wallerstein, *Dynamics of Global Crisis*, New York 1982, pp. 108 ff. In 1972 he had predicted the economic downturn to come, in an article in Italy translated years later in English: 'Towards a Theory of Capitalist Crisis', *New Left Review* I/111, September–October 1978, pp. 3–24. For Arrighi's recollections of that time, see 'The Winding Paths of Capital', *New Left Review* 56, March–April 2009, pp. 65–8.

and consent. But unlike his contemporaries, Arrighi located its crux not in ideology, but the economy. Internationally, the condition of hegemony was a superior model of organisation, production and consumption, inducing not only compliance with the ideals and values of the hegemon, but generalised imitation of it as a model among other states. In turn, such hegemony yielded benefits to the ruling groups of all states, by setting predictable rules for the international system and policing common threats to it. Hegemony in this sense was to be contrasted with mere 'exploitative domination', in which a powerful state extorts obedience or tribute from others by the exercise of violence, without conferring compensating benefits on them. Within a state or between states, hegemony was 'the additional power that accrues to a dominant group by virtue of its capacity to place all the issues around which conflict rages on a "universal" plane'. Internationally, that meant the leadership accruing to any state that could 'credibly claim to be the motor force of a general expansion of the collective powers of rulers vis-a-vis subjects' or 'can credibly claim that the expansion of its power relative to some or even all other states is in the general interest of the subjects of all states'.[38] Typically, such claims were realised not just by a management but a transformation of the pre-existing system of states, ushering in a novel combination of capitalism and territorialism—the independent but interlocking dynamics of capital accumulation at the level of the enterprise, and spatial expansion at the level of the state.

Such is the analytic framework for the succession of world-historical hegemonies tracked in *The Long Twentieth Century*. After the proto-hegemonies of the city-states of Venice and Genoa in Renaissance Italy, Arrighi's narrative moves to the

---

38 *The Long Twentieth Century: Money, Power and the Origins of Our Times*, London–New York 1994, pp. 28, 30.

three great hegemonies, as he saw them, of the modern age: first of the Dutch Republic in the seventeenth, then of Britain in the nineteenth, and finally of the United States in the twentieth century.[39] Driving this sequence forward are cycles of capital accumulation, under the sign of Marx's formula M-C-M'. Capitalist expansion, whose most advanced firms are concentrated in the hegemon, is initially material—investment in the production of goods and conquest of markets. But over time competition drives down profits, since any one bloc of capital cannot control the space in which rival blocs develop techniques or products that force down final prices. At that point, accumulation in the hegemon—and more generally—switches over to financial expansion, as rival states compete for mobile capital in their drive for territorial aggrandisement. With intensifying rivalry, and the outbreak of military conflicts, hegemony breaks down, issuing into a period of systemic chaos. Out of this chaos, a new hegemonic power ultimately emerges, restarting a cycle of material expansion on a new foundation, capable of serving the interests of all other states, and some or all of the interests of their subjects. In this sequence, each successive hegemony has been more comprehensive, enjoying a wider and a more powerful base than the last—the Dutch Republic was still a

---

39 The addition of Dutch hegemony to the sequence, absent from *The Geometry of Imperialism*, is testimony to the fruitful interaction between Arrighi and Wallerstein. The word hegemony is not to be found in the first volume of the latter's *The Modern World-System* (1974). In the second (1980), it is defined as the simultaneous superiority of one core power over all others in production, commerce and finance—flanked in the Dutch case by maritime power, scientific and technological advance, a soupçon of social mobility, and higher wages than elsewhere, allowing a balance of interests between owners and producers undergirding the state. See *The Modern World System*, II, pp. 38–9, 61–71, 113. By the time of the fourth volume (2011), dedicated to the memory of Arrighi, hegemony requires no exposition—it is taken for granted, Wallerstein remarks: p. xii.

hybrid between a city-state and a nation-state, Britain was a nation-state, the US is a continental state.

Where in this history were we now? Very early, Arrighi held that the post-war material expansion of capitalism under American hegemony had petered out at the end of the sixties, and that since the crisis of the seventies, it had given way to a cycle of financial expansion, exploited by the US to retain its world power beyond its time.[40] Arrighi predicted, again very early, that this financial expansion would be unsustainable, and that with its eventual implosion would come a terminal crisis of American hegemony. What lay ahead? Writing in 1994, Arrighi observed that an unprecedented aspect of the foreseeable twilight of American hegemony, quite unlike the dusk of Dutch or British hegemony, was that a bifurcation between military power and financial power had opened up, since America still retained an overwhelming global predominance of armed force, even while sinking to the status of a debtor nation as the cashbox of the world moved to East Asia. Nothing quite like this had happened before. Did it mean that with the passing of a hegemon another time of systemic chaos lay ahead?

Not necessarily. In his later work, Arrighi dallied with the idea the world might finally be able to escape the logic of capital and cycles of hegemony, with their destructive aftermaths. Braudel had taught that capitalism was not to be equated with production for the market—it was a superstructure of finance erected above it, requiring state power for its operations. Might then a market society as Smith, no friend of merchant greed or colonial aggression, had once envisaged it, offer an egalitarian

---

40 Here an important influence on him came from David Calleo, a conservative thinker whose *Beyond American Hegemony* (1987) offered a striking historical critique of hegemonic-stability theory, and the Anglo-American apologetics associated with it, from which Arrighi took the concept of 'exploitative domination' that figures significantly in his own work.

alternative to capital as Marx had depicted it? In pre-modern times, did distinctive patterns of East Asian development before the arrival of Western imperialism foreshadow the practicability of such a path? Could the spectacular growth of the People's Republic in the new century, with an economy larger than that of the US in sight, have its roots in a recovery of the dynamics of that earlier epoch?[41] In the end, only tentative answers were possible, but it was in this direction—'the emergence of an East Asia-centred world market society based on the mutual respect of the world's cultures and civilisations', and a 'socially and ecologically sustainable model of development'—that Arrighi's final hopes lay.[42]

They had a logic in a gap in the execution of his original project. Labour—central to the synthesis he had planned in the mid-seventies, before moving to the US—was missing in *The Long Twentieth Century*. It had proved too difficult, he remarked, to accommodate in a structure dominated by the dynamics of financialisation, of which he had little sense in that earlier time.[43] But when he came to write his sequel, *Adam Smith in Beijing*, it was still absent. Behind the lacuna lay a disappointment. He had seen the working class of the West at the peak of its post-war unruliness, in the turbulent Italy of the sixties and early seventies, and as he worked on *The Long Twentieth Century* had not lost his deep commitment to the global fate of labour. Four years before the book appeared, he published an arresting reconstruction of its history since *The Communist Manifesto*. For Marx the future of the working class as the gravedigger of capitalism lay in its combination of the collective power conferred

41 *Adam Smith in Beijing*, London-New York 2007, pp. 24–39, 57–63, 314–36.
42 Postscript to the 2010 edition of *The Long Twentieth Century*, p. 385.
43 'The Winding Paths of Capital', pp. 73–4. It fell to his partner Beverly Silver to tackle the other side of the story, in her *Forces of Labor*, New York 2003.

on it by modern industry, and the social misery inflicted on it by
the pauperising logic of capitalist production for profit—a posi-
tivity making it capable of overthrowing the power of capital,
and a negativity impelling it do so.

But what Marx had joined, history separated. Where
advanced industry maximised the objective social power of
labour, in Scandinavia and the Anglosphere, and after the war
Western Europe and Japan, workers chose Bernstein's path of
reformism. Where levels of economic development were low,
in Russia and elsewhere in the East, material misery created
the subjective conditions for Lenin's road to revolution. Since
the downturn of the seventies, however, both destinations had
entered into crisis, as outsourcing to the South weakened the
working class of the West, and industrialisation strengthened
the working class of the East, starting to reshuffle the constituents of labour that had remained polarised for so long.
Solidarność in Poland and strike waves in Korea or Brazil
were signs of a global levelling of conditions that held out the
possibility of something like Marx's vision coming true.[44]

Another decade of neo-liberalism later—Solidarność vanished, unionisation in free fall across the West—was that still
likely? *Chaos and Governance in the Modern World System*,
co-authored with Beverly Silver, was more cautious, but not
downcast. True, a 'labour-unfriendly international regime' was
now in place, but might not Polanyi's counter-movement of
resistance to commodification be at work too? After all, social
democrats were in office in thirteen out of fifteen states of the
European Union. 'The disempowerment of social movements—
the labour movement in particular—that has accompanied the
global financial expansion of the 1980s and 1990s is largely a

44 'Marxist Century, American Century: The Making and Remaking of the
World Labour', *New Left Review* I/179, January–February 1990, pp. 29–63.

conjunctural phenomenon', Arrighi and Silver decided, predicting the likelihood of a new wave of social conflicts to
come.[45] There is an echo of this expectation in *Adam Smith
in Beijing*, which touches briefly on rural and urban unrest in
China, but it is relatively faint and marginal to the argument of
the book.

In part, the sources of this inflection in Arrighi's thought lay
in its original matrix in Italy. The group he led in the early seventies formed part of the broad stream of *operaismo*, an important
current of which—Mario Tronti its most influential theorist—
looked with admiration at the achievements of American labour
in the fortress of Fordism under the far-sighted rule of FDR.
Inheriting an overestimation of the New Deal from this Italian
tradition, Arrighi attributed to American hegemony, at its
height, a capacity to project outwards a model of global welfare
along the lines of the New Deal, as if Washington had indeed
responded to 'the general interest of the subjects of all states'.
In forgetting his own caveat that 'the claim of the dominant
group to represent a universal interest is always more or less
fraudulent',[46] a miscalculation of what the CIO and UMW had
gained prepared the way for the later turn of his gaze away from
labour. At the same time, in his repertoire of political experience, there was always another force of rebellion, and wellspring
of political change, which he had witnessed in Salisbury and
Dar es Salaam, and for which he never lost a very strong feeling.
Global inequality between states was, after all, far greater than
between classes in the advanced states of the West. The Third
World would not be subordinated so easily. The predictions of

---

45 *Chaos and Governance in the Modern World System*, Minneapolis 1999,
    pp. 12–13, 282.
46 'The Three Hegemonies of Historical Capitalism', *Review (Fernand Braudel
    Center)*, Summer 1990, p. 367.

Marx had not come to pass in Detroit, but the intuitions of Smith might be taking shape in Beijing.

His early formation had another effect on his later work. Unlike the general run of *operaismo*, his group was expressly Gramscian. But in its theorisation of 'workers' autonomy', it laid principal stress not on Gramsci's notebooks, but his writing on factory councils in the *Ordine Nuovo* phase of his career, before his imprisonment. Reacting against PCI instrumentalisation of the prison writings, it had little time for the 'national-popular' themes in them, an object of outright scorn in other sectors of *operaismo*. This left its trace in Arrighi. Building Gramsci's ideas outwards from the national plane of classes to the international system of states, he transformed Gramsci's legacy more radically and creatively than anyone. But though the resulting architectonic included both levels, there was no doubt which predominated. The system came first; the states composing it, a long way second. 'Our interest in unit-level processes', *Chaos and Governance* remarks, 'is strictly limited to the role they play as a source of systemic change in hegemonic transitions.'[47] Nations were thus always the weak link in his Gramscian construction, the structures of hegemonic power within them rarely achieving much salience. That could lead to insouciance, the rulers of America and China alike—paladins of the New Deal or the Reform Era—benefitting from a brush too broad to capture them, or the detail of their talons on those below them.

In transporting to such great effect Gramsci's conception of hegemony from the intra-state to the inter-state plane, there was a related cost. Arrighi was aware of Guha's work, regularly citing it in his depiction of the decline of US power in the world, which too had become 'domination without

---

47   *Chaos and Governance*, pp. 35–6.

hegemony'.[48] But there is difference between the two planes. Relations between classes within a nation are contained with a legal and cultural framework common to them that does not exist between states. The organic composition of hegemony, in Guha's terms, is thus always distinct in international politics, with a far higher ratio of coercion to persuasion than in domestic politics. Wars remain a classic medium of relations between states—seven of them are currently waged by a Nobel Peace laureate—and today sanctions form their scarcely less coercive complement. Historically, the resort to military force Arrighi took to be a sign that American hegemony had passed was a traditional exercise of it; while its correlate in economic blockade has never been so successful. That his timing might be out does not mean his prognosis will prove wrong. Missing, nevertheless, in an opinion so generally held, has always been some safeguard against a wish becoming father to the thought.

---

48   *Chaos and Governance*, pp. 27, 243–5; *Adam Smith in Beijing*, pp. 15–151, 178.

9

INVERSION

There is only one country in today's world where hegemony is a central term in the official language of the state. In China alone can it be found even in the constitution. The irony of its arrival at that position casts a paradoxical—sharply, if obliquely, germane—light on its fortunes in the West, in a history stretching back further even than its emergence in classical Greece. When the Western Zhou kingdom collapsed after three hundred years in the eighth century BC, the realm of its Eastern Zhou successor became a patchwork of contending feudal lords under a royal authority that was increasingly nominal, surrounded by a still only semi-sinicised periphery. In these conditions, there arose in the seventh century the figure of a lord commanding superior force, and the support of lesser lords, in formal protection of the realm against external or internal threats to it, and invested *ex post facto* in this role by the king—the first designated by the new term *ba*, the second by the traditional title *wang*. The *ba*—legend would have it that over time there were five of them, a magical number—headed leagues composed of their allies, held assemblies of them, solemnised pacts and oaths between them. The resemblance of this pattern to the leagues of classical

Greece led Western historians, quite early on, to render the term
ba as a 'hegemon'.[1]

As the house of Zhou became ever more vestigial, and
regional lords amassed territory and troops to create fully-
fledged states locked in rivalry with each other, by the time of
Confucius in the sixth century the *ba* had vanished from the
scene. But the memory of them lived on through the anarchy of
the Warring States period over the next two hundred and fifty
years, when China was divided into a set of predator military
polities engaged in continual battles with each other, and scholars dismayed by this scene sought remedies for it in idealised
images of the lost unity of the past, when the Zhou empire was
integral and uncontested across the land. In such a value-order,
the *ba* could not readily fit, since they already spoke dilution
and division of what should be one and unimpaired. Confucius
was still ambivalent about them. Asked what he thought of Guan
Zhong, the ruthless right hand-man of the first *ba*, he hedged:
'With Guan Zhong as his prime minister, Duke Huan was able
to become hegemon and impose order on the realm. Even to
this day people benefit from what he did'. But pressed as to his
moral qualities, he could only sigh: 'As for his benevolence,
his benevolence …'[2]

Two centuries later, amid the chaos of the Warring States,
Mencius was categorical: the *ba* were an abomination, even if
those who had come after them were still worse: 'A hegemon
uses force to feign benevolence. He must have a large state to
begin with. A king is virtuous and practices benevolence. He

---

1   This seems to have occurred quite independently in successive European
    languages: compare Edward Parker, *Ancient China Simplified*, London
    1908, pp. 33, 38, 72, 97; Henri Maspero, *La Chine antique*, Paris 1927, pp.
    245–9 ff.; Otto Franke, *Geschichte des chinesischen Reiches*, Bd I, Berlin
    1930, pp. 160–2 ff.
2   *Analects*, Book 14: 18, 15.

does not require the possession of a large state ... A hegemon subdues others by force, but they do not voluntarily obey him; they submit because they are weaker. A king commands obedience by his virtue, and the people are happy and sincere in giving him homage'—adding, to make matters absolutely clear: 'The five hegemons were criminals in comparison with the three dynasties.'[3]

With this, a stark dichotomy was set: the principles of a *ba* were deceit and violence, the principles of a *wang* were humanity and benevolence—*ren*, the cardinal Confucian virtue. At the beginning of the third century BCE, Xunzi was more nuanced. Since contemporary rulers were morally much lower than even the *ba*, a typology of power had to be a trichotomy, to include now the figure of a *qiang*, a mere strongman. 'A king seeks to acquire the right men. A hegemon seeks to acquire allies. A strongman seeks to acquire territory'. Whereas a *qiang* simply ruled by brute force, incurring the hatred of others and his own self-destruction, a *ba* could play a relatively constructive economic and political role, if a true *wang* were lacking. On the other hand, it was shameful actually to praise hegemons, who 'did not govern through education', failed to 'pursue culture and good order', used 'deference as a cover for conflict', and 'gave the appearance of benevolence, while walking the path of profit'. They were a *pis-aller*. Xunzi, though a much more realistic thinker than Confucius or Mencius, relapsed to standard pieties in extolling their opposite: 'The true king is not like this. His benevolence is the loftiest in the world. His righteousness is the loftiest in the world. His authority is the loftiest in the world ... There is no one in the world who fails to have affection for him. With an authority that cannot be resisted, he gains victory without battle and acquires territory without attack. Without

---

3   *Mengzi*, Books 2A, 3:1, and 6B, 7:1.

labours of weapons or armour, the whole world submits to him.'[4]

---

4   *Xunzi*, 9: 139–41; 7 37–48, ; 9, 203–2011. The contradictions in Xunzi's depiction of the hegemon are typical across the range of pre-Qin texts. Most of these were no doubt due to the way they were composed or preserved: either—as in the case of the *Analects*, the *Mencius*, and still more blatantly, the later *Guanzi*—entirely the product of different writers after the death of their supposed authors, or—as in the case of the *Xunzi* and the *Han Feizi*—subject to later interpolation. Stylistic analyses to separate out the various layers of the canon seem yet to have been undertaken. In all probability, in some cases the contradictions may have been a function of the different power-holders to whom the literati of the time, from Confucius onwards, addressed themselves, in hope of position as advisers. Sima Qian's portrait of Lord Shang (Gongsun Yang), a figure later handed down to posterity as the theorist of a ruthless Legalism, offers a nice illustration of this ductility, in recounting his efforts to become counselor to Duke Xiao of Qin, the great grandfather of the First Emperor. 'Duke Xiao granted Gongsun Yang an interview, and Yang talked to him at length. Duke Xiao now and then dozed off, not even listening. When the interview was over, the duke remarked angrily to Jing Jian, "That visitor of yours is a mere impostor! What use could a man like that be?" Jing Jian thereupon berated Gongsun Yang, but Yang said, "I discoursed to the duke on the way of an emperor (*didao*), but it did not seem to take his fancy". Five days later, Jing Jian asked the duke to see Yang once more. Yang had an interview with him and spoke with even greater fervour, though he still failed to interest the duke. After the interview, the duke again complained to Jing Jian, and Jing Jian in turn berated Yang. Yang said, "I discoursed to the duke on the way of a king (*wangdao*), but it did not appeal to him. I would like to be granted another interview". When Yang was granted another interview, the duke expressed approval, but was still unwilling to employ him. When the interview was over and Yang had withdrawn, Duke Xiao said to Jing Jian, "That visitor of yours is a good man—someone worth talking to!" Yang explained to Jing Jian, "I discoursed to the duke on the way of a hegemon (*badao*). It seems as though he would like to try it out. I will know what to say this time!" When Yang appeared to him for another interview, the duke talked with him, inching forward until before he knew it he was kneeling at the very edge of his mat. They talked for several days without tiring. Jing Jian said, "How did you manage to impress our ruler so? He is overjoyed!" Gongsun Yang said, "I discoursed to the ruler on the ways of the emperor and the king, such as were in use in the Three Dynasties of old. But he said, "That takes too much time. I can't wait that long. A worthy ruler is one who can make himself famous throughout the world in his own lifetime. Who can sit around fretting for 30 or 40 or 100 years

What did he have to do to achieve this miracle? 'He who cultivates ritual (*li*) will become a true king.'[5] Amid the violence of the times, there crystallised the counter-image of a pacified realm, governed by suasion in the person of a sage-king, embodying moral authority and practical wisdom, able to unite 'all under heaven' (*tianxia*). Since there was no principle of religious transcendence in the Chinese thought-world to which an appeal could be made as an ultimate criterion of value, a mythicised historical past—the golden age of the 'Three Dynasties'—came to function as a substitute, serving from the time of Confucius onwards as an imaginary absolute. In this rear-view fixation, power was frictionless: so long as the rites were observed and ranks respected once again, society would be at one with its ruler.

It was left to the most powerful mind of the age, from the entirely distinct tradition of Legalism, to leave such superstitions behind. For Han Feizi, the past was no standard of excellence: humanity had once been mere gatherers of fruits and berries, without even use of fire for cooking. Precedent was no basis for knowledge or action.[6] The cult of the Three Dynasties was mindless, and obsession with ritual futile. The enlightened

---

in hopes of becoming an emperor or a king?" Therefore I discoursed to the ruler on the techniques for strengthening the state, and the ruler was pleased. Of course, it will still be hard for him to equal the virtue of the Yin or Zhou dynasties": *Records of the Grand Historian: Qin Dynasty* (tr Burton Watson), Hong Kong 1993, pp. 90–1.

5   *Xunzi*, 9:122,

6   'There was a farmer of Song who tilled the land and in his field there was a stump. One day a rabbit, racing across the field, bumped into the stump, broke its neck and died. Thereupon the farmer laid aside his plough and took up watch beside the stump, hoping he would get another rabbit in the same way. But he got no rabbits and became the laughing stock of Song. Those who think they can take the ways of ancient kings and use them to govern the people of today belong in the category of stump-watchers': *Han Feizi*, 49.

ruler 'has little time for extolling the ancients. Therefore he does not talk about benevolence and righteousness.'[7] A generation younger than Xunzi, from an aristocratic family, Han Feizi discarded Xunzi's trichotomy of *wangdao*, *badao* and *qiangdao*—the way of the king, the way of the hegemon, and the way of the strongman—for *zhudao* or simply, 'the way of the sovereign', fusing Legalism and Daoism in a theory of rule that integrated violence and ideology, coercion and consent, into a single, interlocking system. In this synthesis, it was the impersonal authority of the law—at once compulsion and indoctrination—not the magical effects of ritual that secured the obedience of the people; and *wuwei* (non-action), vigilantly applied, that ensured control of the officials executing it.[8] In a memorial to Yingzheng, ruler of Qin before he became the First Emperor of China, Han Feizi urged him to attack the 'vertical alliance' of states on the central plain that pretended to *tianxia*, and thereby to achieve supremacy as a personification of what previous scholars had polemically separated and counterposed. He should aim to become a *bawang*—that is, a ruler combining the force of a hegemon with the suasion of a king.

The King of Qin, after he unified China, preferred the new title that he invented for himself, *huangdi*—Emperor. But when the Qin empire collapsed after his death, Xiang Yu, the rebel general who occupied its capital, proclaimed himself not emperor but *bawang*, before he was defeated and killed by a rival who founded the Han empire. Under the new dynasty,

---

7   *Han Feizi*, 50.

8   'The way of the sovereign is to treasure stillness and reserve … So still he seems to be nowhere at all; so empty no one can seek him out. Be empty, still and idle and from your place of darkness observe the defects of others. See but do not appear to be seen, listen but do not seem to listen; know but do not let it be known that you know': *Han Feizi*, 1—a typical Daoist passage that is a verse in the original.

the ideological legacy of its predecessor was not abruptly suppressed, as the First Emperor had (reportedly) repressed teachings of *ru*, but evolved into a looser syncretism of Legalist and Daoist elements, with some strands of Confucianism, in what became known as Huang-Lao thinking, which found political expression in the hotchpotch compilation of the so-called *Guanzi*, mythically ascribed to Guan Zhong, adviser to Duke Huan five hundred years earlier, most of it composed in the second and finally collated at the end of the first century BC. In it, *wang* and *ba* recur in the kind of formulaic procession to be found in Xunzi, if now the third term of the trio (or quartet) is no longer *qiang* at the end, but can be *di*—emperor—at the beginning, as befitted post-Qin times. In such passages, the ambiguity around *ba* in Xunzi has disappeared: no negative aura attaches to the hegemon.[9] Other passages lay down common conditions of rule for kings and hegemons alike, before specifying particulars for each. In others again, the two terms merge into the compound *bawang*, as in Han Feizi.[10]

But as the Han state gradually found a new equilibrium, based on lower taxation and larger landlords, scholar gentry balancing court and army, Confucian ideology—designed for and naturally congenial to the literati—came to shroud and envelop a continuing core of Legalist practice, inherited from

---

9 Eg: 'The emperor (*di*) avoids action. The king (*wang*) acts, but without deliberate purpose. The hegemon (*ba*) acts, but not for honours. The prince (*gui*) avoids action designed to honour himself. That is the way of rulers. To seek honours in moderation is the way of the minister (*chen*)'; or 'The treasure of a king is spent on his people; of a hegemon on his generals and troops; of a weak ruler on those in high position, of a doomed ruler on women and precious stones'. *Guanzi*, I, 5; IV, 12.

10 For such usages, see especially *Guanzi*, IX. 23: 'Ba Yan'—'Conversations of a Hegemon', probably a title misplaced from 'Ba Xing'—'Conditions of a Hegemon'—which precedes it, for which see Allyn Rickett's commentary in his unfinished translation of the *Guanzi*, Princeton 1985, pp. 348–55.

the Qin. In this synthesis, the 'hundred schools' of the Warring States—and Huang-Lao too—were slowly relegated to limbo by Confucian orthodoxy, with the canonisation of its doctrines of *ru*. But it was a gradual process. In the mid first century BCE, the Emperor Xuan could still rebuke his heir for thinking it was possible to rule the empire just by rituals, rather than a combination of *badao* and *wangdao*;[11] and the hybrid *bawang* persisting in occasional neutral or laudatory use down through Tang times and beyond.

With the rise of Neo-Confucianism in the late twelfth century, all this changed. Under the Northern Song, rival forces at the imperial court had taken a pragmatic view of the distinction between king and hegemon: the reform statesman Wang Anshi accepting devaluation of the latter, but contending that the former should not be held to ancient standards that were no longer realistic, while his conservative opponent, the historian Sima Guang, argued that *wang* and *ba* had simply been designations of rank, without moral overtones, each applying the same methods of government.[12] With the expulsion of the dynasty above the Yangzi by the Jürchen, and its retrenchment in the south, followed by widespread questioning among the literati as to what had gone wrong, the strain in Confucianism

---

11 Mark Edward Lewis, *Writing and Authority in Early China*, Albany 1999, pp. 351, 493: 'When [the heir-apparent] had grown up, he was soft and benevolent, and loved the *ru* ... Once while attending on [Emperor Xuan] at a banquet, he urged, "Your majesty wields punishments too greatly, you ought to employ the *ru* scholars". Emperor Xuan scowled and said: The Han house has its own institutions, based on the mixing of the way of kings and that of hegemons. How can we simply rely on transformation through virtue, and use Zhou policies?'

12 See Peter Bol, *'This Culture of Ours': Intellectual Transitions in T'ang and Song China*, Stanford 1992, pp. 227, 229. The foremost literary figure of the period, the poet-statesman Su Shih, relativised the distinction in another way—rulers should act as kings or hegemons according to their personal capacities: pp. 265–6.

that made into an abstract metaphysical moralism, hostile both to practical statecraft and to aesthetic sensibility, gained the upper hand. Systematised by Zhu Xi, the leader of the turn, *dao xue*—'True Way'—doctrine counterposed principles to results, giving for the first time canonical status to Mencius as one of the Four Books on which the examination system would come to be based, and thereby making condemnation of the *ba* irremediable. The cultivation of virtue was not to be contaminated by pursuit of benefits, which stemmed from self-interest, and could yield nothing positive. Guanzi's supposed achievements had proved short-lived, and later rulers, more or less all tainted by Legalism, had degenerated still further.

In his lifetime, Zhu Xi's doctrine met vigorous resistance. His leading intellectual opponent, Chen Liang, placed social results squarely before personal qualities. Not just Guanzi, shrouded in the mists of legend, but the founders of the Han and Tang dynasties, Gaozu and Taizong—each of whom had famously waded through violence and treachery to seize power—were heroic figures, embodying at once the way of the king and the way of the hegemon, who had conferred historic benefits on society. It made no sense to counterpose the methods of *wang* and *ba*: every successful rule rested on a balance between the two. Shocked to find that among students in Zhejiang a 'gang of scoundrels with scurrilous tongues advocate despising the king and honouring the *ba*, contemplating advantage and calculating results', Zhu warned Chen against the fatal attempt to combine integrity and utility.[13] It was the last such exchange for a long time. In 1238 an imperial decree made Zhu Xi's system— officially renamed *li xue*, School of Principles—state orthodoxy, and he himself an object of worship in the Confucian temple.

---

13 Hoyt Tillman, *Utilitarian Confucianism, Chen Liang's challenge to Chu Hsi*, Cambridge MA, 1982, pp. 182–3.

In 1313 his Four Books—Mencius subsequently purged of inconvenient passages—became the basis of the examination system. Henceforth, there could be no ambivalence. *Ba* became a synonym for self-interest and violence, *wangdao* and *badao* a polarity of good and evil, their connotations sinking into popular language itself, where *ba* became a colloquial term for a bully and *bawang* could feature in *The Dream of the Red Chamber* of the mid-eighteenth century—its second term compounding rather than counterbalancing the pejorative sense of the first—as the sobriquet of Baochai's reprehensible brother, the louche Xue Pan.

II

The enthronement of the School of Principles as a doctrine of state did not reduce Confucian culture in Ming-Qing China to Zhu Xi's system. Literature could thrive, surviving his contempt for it, alternative philosophical outlooks find expression, and new disciplines—essentially a more historically-minded philology—emerge. But political thought was sterilised, ideological conformity to a Neo-Confucian order of static moralistic abstraction re-enforced by heightened repression and censorship with the advent of the Manchu.

In Japan of the same period, Confucian scholarship took altogether another direction. There, since the twelfth century, warriors rather than officials had ruled, in a feudal society with a figurehead imperial line, but no centralised bureaucratic state, where supreme political power was held by a succession of shoguns, the highest warlords in the land. After 150 years of internecine strife, the Tokugawa Shogunate had by the early seventeenth century pacified the country and established a stable *baku-han* regime, in which Confucian ideas could for the first time take significant native root. The setting in which they did so differed radically, however, from that in China. There was no examination system, no ancestor-worship, no Confucian temples. Traditionally, legitimation of power was supplied by Buddhism, far more entrenched than in China, or Shintoism. Confucian intellectuals—typically *déclassés* doctors, monks or samurai—thus started from marginal positions, and could also become vulnerable to charges of an unpatriotic sinocentrism. Still, Chinese culture had always enjoyed high prestige in Japan, and they could draw on a body of learning that was larger and more sophisticated than any rival in bidding for influence with the Bakufu, which gradually—by the time of the fourth or fifth Tokugawa shogun—integrated them into its rule, if never according them the status their Chinese counterparts held. At the same time, because there was no bureaucratic centralisation of power in Japan, they were also structurally in many ways freer than the Chinese literati. For the Bakufu was not only flanked by an imperial court that, though practically impotent, retained symbolical aura, but also directly controlled no more than a third of the country, the rest forming fiefs of *daimyō*, each with their own revenues and warriors, owing allegiance to, but running their domains independently of, the shogun. In due course, moreover, the feudal order in Japan permitted a much more dynamic merchant culture in Edo and Osaka than the Qing autocracy allowed in the cities of China. In this more variegated landscape, the space for independent thought was significantly greater.

In these conditions, Confucians were faced with political questions for which their sources in China offered little obvious guidance. Unity of the realm was an absolute value in the classical Chinese canon, which from Qin times onwards had taken practical shape in a centralised imperial state. But if division of the realm could never be accepted, overthrow of a dynasty could. The mandate of heaven could be forfeited. It was a lease, not an irrevocable title to power, transferrable after the fact to a successful rebellion. The configuration in Japan was just the opposite. Sovereignty was divided between a military ruler in formal command of the country and a vestigial emperor, theoretically delegating power to him. The imperial line, on the other hand, might be impotent but it was unbroken. Chinese emperors styled themselves Sons of Heaven, but the title was metaphorical: no one took it literally, heaven itself remaining an abstraction. Japanese emperors, by contrast, were—in official mythology; biologically they were of Korean descent—progeny of the coupling of the goddess Amaterasu with her brother. This numinous religious origin made actual replacement, as opposed to neutralisation, of them effectively taboo. How was this combination—the inherent tension of a divided sovereignty—to be theorised? For Confucians, ready to hand was the dichotomy of king and hegemon—in Japanese, *ō* and *ha*. Should these be mapped onto emperor and shogun? If so, should their valences be preserved or modified? Or was divided sovereignty itself an anomaly that was not to be legitimated, but criticised and overcome?

In wrestling with this set of problems for two hundred years and more of Tokugawa rule, Japanese intellectuals not only generated a livelier and richer corpus of political thought than was possible under the Qing, but necessarily altered the meanings and connotations of *wangdao* and *badao*. At the beginning, the leading scholar of *ru*, Itō Jinsai (1627–1725), who generally avoided questions of statecraft, could not have been more orthodox, declaring: 'The distinction between the true king and the hegemon is the first principle of Confucianism'. More original and political in cast of mind, Ogyū Sorai (1666–1728) pioneered commentary on Han Feizi at a time he was still essentially an *auteur maudit* in China,[14] and attacked Mencius for his moralising contrast between the *wangdao* and *badao*. 'True kings', he wrote, 'differ from hegemons merely because of matters of rank related to their historical epoch'—not according to the humanity or otherwise of their methods of rule. For if hegemons had to exercise coercion, 'that was something' he went on, 'that could not be helped'. For after all, 'Confucius did not even have a one-*shaku* fief, and so was unable to rise to power. Even though a person may be virtuous, how could they avoid resorting to force?'[15]

Sorai, who expressed a low opinion of the cultural level of the country's military rulers past and present, with the exception of the Tokugawa founder Ieyasu, as 'uneducated', did not offer an explicit justification of the Bakufu on this basis—*ha* remained too delicate a term to apply to the Shogun. But since he made it clear he regarded the imperial line as politically defunct, and his criteria for the exercise of power were resolutely consequentialist, critics had no hesitation in attacking him as little better than 'a Confucian hegemon' himself, like the *ha* feigning benevolence to spread subversion.[16] That, his unpublished treatise on government, containing much that was unsettling about social ills of the time, might well have been thought to risk: not least his warning that 'although the *daimyō* are all vassals of the shogun, some may inwardly tend to regard the emperor as their true sovereign, since their titles are granted as imperial charters and their letters of appointment issued by the court.

---

14 See Bertil Lundahl, *Han Feizi: The Man and the Work*, Stockholm 1992, p. 88.

15 *Ogyū Sorai's Philosophical Masterworks: The Bendo and Benmei*, Honolulu 2006, pp. 334–7, dismissing Mencius's denunciations of hegemons as the misrepresentations of a polemicist. The influence of Sima Guang is plain, and perhaps Chen Liang too.

16 See Tucker's introduction to *Ogyū Sorai's Philosophical Masterworks*, p. 80.

If they continue to feel they are vassals of the shogun simply for fear of his power, trouble may come in the years ahead'.[17] Following Sorai, his pupil Dazai Shundai (1680–1747) held that Mencian precepts were fine as a political diet in ordinary times, but for illnesses strong medicine was needed, requiring recipes from Legalism, when not *wangdao* but *badao* could best serve the primary function of all government, to secure the material well-being of the people. The imperial line was a mere 'dangling thread', incapable of the task of answering social needs; a shogun who did so merited the title of 'famed ruler'.

These were thinkers who never enjoyed any real proximity to power. Arai Hakuseki (1657–1725), on the other hand, was part of the inner apparatus of the Bakufu as an adviser to the sixth and seventh Tokugawa shoguns. Unconcerned with exegesis of classic texts, he composed instead a political history of Japan from mediaeval times, in which successive predecessors of the Tokugawa—Taira, Muromachi, Ashikaga, Oda, Hideyoshi—were treated as so many *ha* who had respected the imperial dynasty, but so emptied it of power that his narrative could essentially ignore the throne. However, in failing to become monarchs themselves, they had perpetuated a bifurcated sovereignty that had no Confucian warrant. How were names to be rectified, so that they corresponded to the reality of things? Hakuseki's solution was to edge the Shogunate towards the kingly status of an *ō*, dispensing with the aura of the imperial court without actually deposing it, since religious authority was still needed, once the power of the monasteries had been broken. Yet that posed its own problem, since in the

---

17 *Discourse on Government* (*Seidan*), Wiesbaden 1999, pp. 192–3, tr. modified. Sorai ended this text: 'I have not even allowed my students to take down this narration. I have written it out myself, using my old eyes and my humble brush. After the shogun has deigned to peruse it, I wish it to be consigned to the flames.'

Confucian world order after the Qin, a king was the ruler of a peripheral kingdom—Korea or Siam—who owed tribute to the emperor in China: a status unacceptable to any Tokugawa, and to Hakuseki himself, for whom Japan as the Land of the East held precedence over any other.[18] The eighth shogun dropped any attempt to bring the protocols of *ha* and *ō* together in the canopy of the Bakufu.

In the opposite direction, Yamagata Daini (1725–1767) lamented the condition of the 'fallen house' of the *tennō*, a 'virtual prisoner' in Kyoto, unable even to tour his provinces. Citing Confucius—'Heaven does not have two suns, a people does not have two kings'—he asked: 'Which side should we follow? One bestows honours but is poor. The other dispenses wealth but enjoys no prestige. Authority is divided because people cannot gain both. One must be sovereign, the other subject'.[19] The shogunate should assist the dynasty, not expropriate imperial power. *In extremis*, he hinted, such usurpation could provoke a successful rebellion as in China. Matters had not reached that point. But a divided sovereignty was unnatural and unstable. For the realm to be healed, name and thing, title and power, should be reunited around the emperor. Mocked by an upholder of the established order—'The shogun adheres to subject status even though he holds sway over the whole realm.

---

18 Hakuseki's career and thought are the subject of the finest single study of any early modern Japanese thinker in a European language, Kate Wildman Nakai's *Shogunal Politics: Arai Hakuseki and the Premises of Tokugawa Rule*, Cambridge MA, 1988, whose findings are summarised above.

19 See Bob Wakabayashi, *Japanese Loyalism Reconstrued: Yamagata Daini's Ryūshi shinron of 1759*, Honolulu 1999 pp. 133–4. 'Duplicity in serving a ruler is unconscionable and violates the immutable moral tenet of the former sages; duality in exacting labour from subjects shows a lack of benevolence, and the masses would not accept that. Today we revile as "lewd" any woman who gives herself over to two men, but we think nothing of a subject who serves two masters. So there must be many chaste wives and no faithful officials'.

This beautiful Japanese custom, without parallel anywhere, is something you Confucian scholars cannot appreciate. Hold your tongue, follower of alien doctrines!'—Daini was executed by the Bakufu.[20]

Radicalizing Sorai and Shundai, on the other hand, Kaiho Seiryō (1755–1817), rejecting a well-connected samurai background for life as an independent scholar, proceeded to a transvaluation squared of Mencius's dichotomy. The royal way—ōdō—was all very well for a pacified empire, surrounded by no external pressures or dangers: it was fit for an 'unruffled and patient old man'. The hegemonic way—hadō—was required where there was no such security, but an environment of conflict and competition, demanding a very different kind of ruler, one of 'rare intelligence, his talents sharp like the point of a drill, and blindingly bright to the eye'.[21] It alone suited Japan. There, in another unexpected twist, Seiryō assigned the Bakufu to a pensioner position as ō, promoting the daimyō to the potentially or actually dynamic roles of ha. Nor was this reversal and displacement of Confucian signs all. Competition was the lifeblood of the hegemon. But this was not primarily military, it was economic. Not troops or weapons, but manufactures and trade formed the essential medium of rivalry, since wealth was the root of power, and every daimyō should aim to maximise it. Seiryō viewed every social tie—lord and vassal, master and servant, buyer and seller—as an economic exchange. The world

20 Matsumiya Kanzan: ibid., p. 135. A quarter of a century later, Fujita Yūkoku of the Mito school offered his gloss on the official position. The Tokugawa were hegemons who acted like kings, but rightly declined any such title themselves: 'For a hegemon to pursue the way of a king—is that not preferable to a king pursuing the way of a hegemon?'

21 See Annick Horiuchi, 'Kaiho Seiryô, or the Importance of Discernment', in W. J. Boot, *Critical Readings in the Intellectual History of Early Modern Japan*, Leiden 2012, pp. 485–6: the outstanding western-language study of Seiryō.

of relations was a universe of commodities and nothing else. 'All under heaven is a merchandise'. Social stratification was a mere product of habit, Confucian rejection of self-interest a cynical ploy for duping the poor. Rites and music were 'children's toys', and moral values utensils for variable use, like so many different pans hanging in a kitchen. A more sweeping reversal of *ru* would be difficult to imagine.

Sorai's teaching had fallen under Bakufu disapproval in the Kansei purge conducted by Matsudaira Sadanobu in 1790, which enforced Zhu Xi's version of Neo-Confucianism as official orthodoxy. Seiryō, a pupil of Shundai, left Edo a year before the crackdown, and for all his audacity, by travelling modestly from place to place in the provinces, writing notes and giving talks, escaped surveillance. After him, heterodoxy would increasingly swerve with more nativist accents towards the imperial pole of reference; culminating at mid century, as discontent with Tokugawa immobilism in the face of Western intrusion mounted, in the full-blown *sonnō jōi*– 'uphold the emperor, expel the barbarian'—ideology of the revolt that toppled the shogunate in 1867.[22] In its last years, the label of *ha* was for the first time widely affixed to it, as an unambiguous stigma. In 1855 the most intellectually gifted of all the young rebels against the inertia of the Bakufu, Yoshida Shōin, delivered a series of lectures on Mencius demanding fundamental change, and invited an elder scholar from his Chōshū *han*, Yamagata Taika, to respond. He was told in reply that 'in our land there are now many who say the Bakufu is a hegemon and that the various *daimyō* are retainers of the imperial court': just what Sorai had feared would one day come to pass. 'This is an error that comes from the insistence of scholars of Chinese learning on using

---

22 Ironically, like much else in the patriotic discourse of the period, the slogan was a line—*zunwang nangyi*—dating from pre-Qin times in China.

terms from ancient China to refer to matters of our country.' In Japan there was on the contrary, as official pronouncements explained, a legitimate delegation of authority from the emperor to the shogun. In Yamagata's words: 'Conditions in our country differ from those in China and here there is no such thing as a *ba*. In China the term *ba* meant one among the various lords who, heading a large, strong state, used its military might to dominate the lords of other states and lead them in a league. The military court of today [sc. the Bakufu] is not just the master of one state; it holds under its authority the lands and the people of the entire realm. It thus cannot be termed a *ba*,' while for their part the *daimyō* were 'all vassals of the shogun who enfeoffed them'. To which Shōin retorted that successive shogunates— numbering five *ba* as in ancient China: Minamoto, Ashikaga, Oda, Hideyoshi, Tokugawa—had acted as hegemons just as Zhu Xi described and condemned these, their culpability mitigated in the case of Hideyoshi alone, who had sincerely revered the emperor.[23] Four years later, Shōin was executed, to be commemorated as a martyr once the Meiji Restoration brought the bifurcation of sovereignty in Japan to an end.

Yet the age-old dichotomy did not expire with it, persisting in two politically opposite afterlives. When the Meiji oligarchs ignored the Charter Oath promise of the Restoration to introduce a constitution and deliberative assembly, a movement for popular rights sprang up in the 1880s, whose outbreaks of revolt they had to put down with force. In the midst of this crisis a homeless young intellectual teaching in a mountain village, Chiba Takusaburō, motivated his detailed draft of a liberal

---

23 *Yoshida Shōin zenshu*, II, Tokyo 1934, pp. 504, 400–1. I owe special thanks to Kate Wildman Nakai for help here, as too for the passage from Fujita Yūkoku above. See also Thomas Huber, *The Revolutionary Origins of Modern Japan*, Stanford 1981, p. 63.

constitution and parliament for the country with a novel version
of *ōdō*—'The Way of the King'. Rejecting 'decadent Confucians
and rural know-nothings' who twisted the Way of the King to
mean absolutist rule by a Louis XIV-style monarch, he turned
the maxim 'the king never dies' into 'the people never die', and
opened his essay by explaining that *ōdō* did not even require a
monarchy—a land without a prince could realise it.[24] Penniless,
he died a year later. The Meiji Constitution, introduced once
unrest had been repressed, would create a political order whose
logic was the antithesis of his hopes.

But in the imperialist expansion over which the new state
presided, *ōdō* would receive its final ideological form in Japan.
From a *han* loyal to the Tokugawa, Nanbu Jirō (1835–1912),
having served as a Meiji consul in China and witnessed the
decay of the Manchu monarchy, started to argue that a common
vision was needed to unify Asia and this was to be found in the
benevolent kingly way, upheld of old in the Confucian classics, rather than the hegemonic path of domination pursued
by the Western powers. His ideas would fascinate a young
military cadet, Ishiwara Kanji (1889–1949), who went on to
become the co-conspirator of the Mukden Incident of 1931 that
launched Japan's seizure of Manchuria, and Chief of Operations
at the General Staff in 1935. Later becoming an opponent of the
Pacific War, he was cashiered for the violence of his attacks on

---

24 'The Way of the King', *Monumenta Nipponica*, Spring 1979, pp. 71,
63; Irokawa Daikichi, *The Culture of the Meiji Period*, Princeton 1985,
p. 104. Takusaburō ended with a postscript: 'You may well ask why I have
written this essay on the Way of the King. Perhaps it is because I am a
little deranged, or perhaps I did it just for amusement. Quite possibly I am
one of those outdated Chinese classicists who know of antiquity but are
ignorant of what is going on today. Or perhaps I am one of those *kokugaku*
scholars who fail to understand politics; they know only the existence of
the imperial house and ignore the existence of the people ... I hope this
essay will serve as a ship to carry them to the shores of understanding'.

Tōjō. The most apocalyptic and maverick mind in the Imperial Army, crossing German *Kriegskunst* with Nichiren Buddhism, in Ishiwara's prolific writing *ōdō* became the uplifting mission of Japan in Manchuria, installing the last Qing emperor Pu Yi as benevolent ruler of the land, and more widely in East Asia at large, marshalling it against the ruthless *hadō* of the hegemons of the West, not to speak of the Soviet Union.[25] A civilian version of the same conception, employing the same dichotomy, came from the former liberal intellectual and journalist Tachibana Shiraki, also active in Manchuria, and became a standard component in the ideological arsenal of the Kwantung Army.[26] Far from abandoning this vision once he was sidelined in 1939, Ishiwara advocated an East Asian League to realise it, whose design incurred the suspicion of the authorities as insufficiently Japanese, at variance with the Co-Prosperity Sphere proclaimed in 1940. When any idea of *ōdō* lay in ruins in 1945, after a war with America he had opposed, he ended up as witness for the defense at the Tokyo trials, pointing out the crimes too, at Hiroshima and Nagasaki, of the *hadō* across the water.

III

In the late-nineteenth and early-twentieth-century China, the space of political thought changed. In classical times, hegemony had come to stand for coercion not persuasion, in a culture whose political thought distinguished the two earlier, more sharply, and more systematically than in the West. But it had done so in

---

25 Mark Peattie, *Ishiwara Kanji and Japan's Confrontation with the West*, Princeton 1975, pp. 33–4, 55–7, 160, 316–29.

26 See Lincoln Li, *The China Factor in Modern Japanese Thought: The Case of Tachibana Shiraki 1881–1945*, Albany 1996, pp. 105–7; and for Tachibana's general role as ideologue of the Kwantung Army in the Japanese occupation of Manchuria, pp. 45–63.

a civilisation without peer competitors. Hegemony remained a notion with an exclusively internal charge: in the absence of any inter-state order, it had no external application. The tributary system, idealised in Confucian fashion as homage of surrounding lands to the imperial authority of the Middle Kingdom, was the conceptual antithesis of it. But once China was quarry to Western imperialism, the term could readily be fastened on its predators.

In 1924 Sun Yat-sen, addressing an audience in Kobe, called on the peoples of Asia to shake off the yoke of Western oppression in a united struggle for their freedom and independence. Two civilisations, he explained, were now locked in conflict. For the past several centuries, European civilisation had been based on a culture of force—aeroplanes, bombs and cannons. In the language of the Ancients, it represented the rule of *badao*, which had always been looked down upon by the Orient. For there was an Asian civilisation superior to it, whose values were 'benevolence, justice and morality', an order that the Ancients had called 'the Kingly Way'—*wangdao*. The contrast between the two was stark. For a thousand years, China had been supreme in the world, a single state as powerful as the United States and Great Britain were today combined. How then did China relate to weaker nations? Did it send its army or navy to force them into submission? Far from it. They sent annual tribute to China of their own free will, regarding it as an honour to be allowed to do so, and shameful if they did not. Under the canopy of the Kingly Way, they went on doing so generation after generation, not only from such lands as Nepal, but even from distant Europe. Today, however, could the peoples of Asia regain their independence by relying on benevolence alone? That was impossible. Japan and Turkey had armed themselves, and the Chinese people too would have to resort to force to avenge their wrongs and win their freedom. In that struggle, the new Russia had separated from the West and joined the East in a common *wangdao*. What of Japan? It had become acquainted with the Western rule of Might, but retained Oriental features of the rule of Right. The question before its people was whether their country would become a hawk and running dog of the West, or a pillar of strength of the East.[27]

In China, as he spoke, the terms he used were already fading. With the fall of the monarchy he had done so much to bring about, invocation of any *wangdao* became obsolete, and with the consolidation of the republic came the abstractions of a modern political vocabulary, altering its opposite in a conceptual shift from person to system in the upper ranges of usage, eliminating the traditional notion of a Way. From hegemon, instead, now came hegemony: *ba* to *baquan*—like its correlate in the West, henceforward the far more usual term. Available in a few little-known Song commentaries on the Spring and Autumn period, this started to crop up after the May Fourth movement against the Versailles Treaty, and by the thirties had a place in political vocabulary, if not a prominent one.

After the Second World War this changed. In 1946, interviewed by Anna Louise Strong, Mao denounced the expansionist drive of the United States to ring the world with its bases as a bid for global hegemony, for the first time tabling *baquan* in

---

27 'Pan-Asianism', in *China and Japan—Natural Friends, Unnatural Enemies*, Shanghai 1941, pp. 141–51. The translation of Sun's speech, which contains various diplomatic omissions—the phrase 'running dog' in its penultimate sentence is suppressed—renders *wangdao* and *badao* as 'rule of Right' and 'rule of Might', except where the former becomes 'the Kingly Way'. The collection in which this translation appeared was a production of Wang Jingwei's collaborationist regime set up by Japan in 1940. It makes full use of Sun's many appeals for help from and expressions of amity towards Japan before his death four months after his speech in Kobe, and concludes with an epilogue from Wang Jingwei hailing 'the common destiny of China and Japan'.

Communist discourse.[28] For some time the term lay fallow in the vocabulary of the People's Republic. But with the eruption of fierce ideological and diplomatic conflict with the Soviet Union during the Cultural Revolution, it came into its own as a designation of the comparable character of the two super-powers of the time, each seen as striving for global hegemony. When the PRC was finally seated at the UN in late 1971, the first address of its delegate to the General Assembly hailed the 'increasing number of medium and small countries' that were uniting to oppose the 'hegemony and power politics of one or two superpowers'. As relations with the USSR worsened, on the first day of 1973 the Chinese people were instructed by Mao—in a variation of advice urged on Zhu Yuanzhang, the fourteenth century founder of the Ming dynasty—to 'dig deep tunnels, store grain everywhere, and never seek hegemony'. In February of the following year, Mao explained that there were three worlds, as widely held in the sixties. But their components had changed. The US and USSR formed the First World; 'middle elements' like Europe, Japan, Canada or Australia, the Second World; while with the exception of Japan all of Asia, Africa and Latin America comprised the Third World.[29] His remarks were swiftly codified in an authoritative commentary as a denun-ciation of *baquanzhuyi* or 'hegemonism', the suffix indicating a semantic escalation. Thereafter the duty to 'combat colonialism,

---

28 'Talk with the American Correspondent Anna Louise Strong', *Selected Works*, Vol. IV, Beijing 1961, p. 100. At that time, the official translation rendered *baquan* as 'domination'.

29 'On the Question of the Differentiation of the Three Worlds', 22 February 1974. The original trio, as initially formulated in France, had been a First World of capitalist states headed by the US, a Second World of communist states headed by the USSR, and a Third World of colonial and semi-colonial countries. After Mao's death, his version was the subject of an unprec-edented complete issue of the *People's Daily*, devoted to its lessons for the fight against the hegemonism of the two superpowers: 1 November 1977.

imperialism and hegemonism' became a watchword of the PRC, reiterated in editorials, speeches, documents and pronouncements from the summit of the state: the central theme of Deng Xiaoping's debut at the United Nations in April 1974, invoking 'the struggle of all peoples against imperialism and particularly against hegemonism', a leitmotif of Zhou Enlai's speech to the National People's Congress the following year, the dangers of hegemonism were written into the 1975 Constitution of the People's Republic itself, where they remain to this day.[30]

In the last years of the Cultural Revolution, all discourse was official discourse. With the arrival of the Reform era, a space for political writing that was less official opened, individual thinkers emerging with their own agendas, some at an angle to directives of the state. From the mid-nineties onwards, conspicuous among these has been Yan Xuetong, who after a doctorate at Berkeley and decade working for a think tank of the Ministry of State Security, now heads the Institute for Modern International Relations at Qinghua University. In the period when he was a student in the United States, at the end of the eighties and early nineties, Deng Xiaoping had reformulated Chinese foreign policy in the wake of the disappearance of the USSR—there was now just one superpower—with a set of directives whose most famous phrase would become 'hide our capabilities and bide our time', which also included the injunction, reiterating Mao's slogan of 1973, 'never seek hegemony.'[31]

---

30   The 1975 and 1978 versions of the Constitution declared that China would uphold 'proletarian internationalism' and resist 'hegemonism'. In the 1982 revision of the charter, presided over by Deng Xiaoping, the former disappeared, but the latter persisted, and sits fast in the latest version of 2004.

31   Often misrepresented as Deng's '24 character instruction', as if it was delivered as such, rather than a later collation by officialdom of remarks at different points of time, including 'observe coolly; secure our position; cope calmly' (September 1989, after the fall of the Berlin Wall); 'China will never claim to be a hegemon' (December 1990, in response to questions whether

For the best part of the next twenty years, the doctrine that it was essential for China to keep a low profile held good in the PRC. Yan sought to offer another and more ambitious agenda. In the new century, China could aim at world leadership. For that, it required a grand strategy and a theory to found one.

The theory he devised set out to fuse the American IR he had absorbed at Berkeley with pre-Qin classics. From the former he took Morgenthau's brand of realism; from the latter, whatever could be put to his purpose. Disavowing any attempt at philological or historical accuracy as scholarship irrelevant to science as pursued by specialists in contemporary international relations, he freely selected, amalgamated and modernised passages and terms from the classical canon at will, in an unspoken adaptation of Sun Yat-sen's schema for the new century. In the restorationist climate of intellectual circles in the nineties, in which nostalgia for the constructive monarchism of the Qing or Yuan Shikai could often be heard, *wangdao* could now stage a comeback as the highest political ideal, 'True Kingship', in Yan's conception. *Badao*, on the other hand, was relativised. Not Mencius's rigid dichotomy, but Xunzi's trichotomy was the appropriate guideline for modern times. Hegemony was inferior to true kingship, but better than *qiangdao* as mere might, sharing some positive features with kingship, appreciated by Xunzi. Both required a solid basis of material—economic and military—power. What set them apart was the factor that Xunzi had rightly seen was decisive: political power, which throughout history commanded the other two. That was, of course, a modern term. But the Ancients had grasped its essence: for them, it lay in 'virtue, benevolence, the Way, justice, law,

it should accept leadership of the Third World); 'hide our capabilities and bide our time' (April 1992, after the fall of the USSR)—or *tao guang yang hui*, a tag dating back to pre-Tang times, the Six Dynasties or earlier.

worthies and sages'—in short, morality.[32] What defined the
superiority of a *wang* over a *ba* was a higher morality: kingly
benevolence over (at best) mere hegemonic reliability. A good
state was then, as it is now, one governed by a sage leader supported by talented ministers.

Internationally, Yan allowed, Xunzi was less far-seeing,
underestimating the degree to which military and economic
power is more important in inter-state than in domestic relations. But he did understand that hierarchy was essential for
order, not only within a society, but between states, whose
different magnitudes have always imposed different responsibilities, from the Five Ordinances of the Western Zhou to the
Security Council of today. Crucially, moreover, his portrayal of
the difference between hegemony and true kingship captured
the contrast between the present role of the United States and
the potential future role of China in the contemporary world.
Unquestionably, America was the global superpower, wielding
a military and economic *baquan* over other nations large and
small.[33] China had yet to match it in such material power, even
if the gap between them was closing. But as it did, what China
should be aiming for was moral leadership. In that decisive
respect, it had made a good start domestically in putting economic before political reform, a priority 'universally accepted
by developing nations', which had given China 'supreme status
in the world in the area of reform'.[34] But the country was still
too inclined to regard the resulting economic success it had
achieved as the key to international leadership, which could

---

32 *Ancient Chinese Thought and Modern Chinese Power*, Princeton 2011, p. 115.

33 By this time, Gramsci had begun to be edited in Chinese, obliging his
principal interpreter Tian Shigang to a neologism, offering *lingdaoquan*—
roughly 'guidance'—in lieu of *baquan* for Gramscian hegemony, a coinage
without further currency.

34 *Ancient Chinese Thought and Modern Chinese Power*, p. 69.

only be political and therefore moral. To make the prospect of China's global primacy more comprehensible—and palatable— to Western audiences, Yan altered his designation of it when he came to publish his ideas in book form, three years after setting them out for Chinese readers. For Occidental consumption, the 'True Kingship' to which the PRC should now aspire was re-baptised 'Humane Authority', and the euphemism transported back into Antiquity.[35] With the advent of Xi Jinping to presi-dency of the People's Republic, calling for a rejuvenation of the country, Yan's hopes of a new and bolder course for his nation rose. No longer confined, he explained for Anglophone readers, to Deng's strategy of keeping a low a profile (dubbed KLP), China had switched to 'striving for achievement' (SFA). The horizon of Humane Authority, when China would displace the hegemon at the helm of the world, beckoned. To reach it, the PRC should abandon its refusal of alliances, seek bases abroad, and prefer military to economic aid for developing countries—yet never seek hegemony, but rather demonstrate moral leadership among the comity of nations, by upholding the banner of the United Nations and international legal norms, and helping to punish those who flout them.[36]

With this construction, a mirror image of Western apolo-gias for American paramountcy was in place. For 'Humane Authority', read 'US Leadership' or in its subsequent recension 'Liberal Hegemony'—*vide* Nye, Hoffman, Ikenberry. Aware of

---

35 Compare the first version of his essay, 'Xunzi's Thoughts on International Politics and Their Implications' in the *Chinese Journal of International Politics*, Winter 2008, pp. 135–65, with the euphemisms of the second version, 'Xunzi's Interstate Political Philosophy and Its Message for Today', in *Ancient Chinese Thought and Modern Chinese Power*, pp. 70–106.

36 See 'From Keeping a Low Profile to Striving for Achievement', *Chinese Journal of International Politics*, Summer 2014, pp. 153–84; 'Q and A: Yan Xuetong Urges China to Adopt a More Assertive Foreign Policy', *New York Times*, 9 February 2016.

the positive valency of the latter description among his inter-
locutors in think-tanks in Europe and America, Yan would
subsequently adjust his terminology again, explaining that his
hope was that China would become 'a new kind of hegemon',[37]
multiplying its friends by its humane conduct and loftier ethical
bearing. The capsizal is not complete, since respective Western
and Eastern claims of a superior value-system have, since the
days of Sun Yat-sen (or at a more ethereal level, Gandhi), never
coincided. Distinctive in Yan's prospectus is the Confucian belief
that thought determines social reality, and morality governs
change, a deep structure in collective mentality that found its
own expression in the Cultural Revolution. In the era of the
Open Door Policy, its version reads: 'The basic cause of shifts
in international power lies in the thought of leaders rather than
in material force'.[38] The moralism of true kingship, however
cross-dressed for foreign eyes, has the same roots. Yan invokes
Morgenthau for his claim to a realism that, immune to Carr's
irony, complaisantly ascribes rather than denies morality to the
exercise of power.

---

37 'Yan Xuetong on Chinese Realism, the Tsinghua School of International
Relations, and the Impossibility of Harmony', *Theory Talks* 51, 2012.
38 *Ancient Chinese Thought and Modern Chinese Power*, p. 67.

10

CROSS-CUTTING

In the West, the interlocking construction of hegemony developed by Arrighi was independently proposed by another thinker on the left at the same point in time. In 1981–1982 Robert Cox, a Canadian who had worked for a quarter of a century in the International Labour Organization, published two essays proposing a new approach to the study of international relations based on the legacy of Gramsci, followed in 1987 by a book-length expansion of his case, *Production, Power and World Order*. Like Arrighi, Cox defined a global hegemony as the outward expansion of the internal hegemony of a dominant social class, unleashing the energies of its rise to power beyond its state boundaries in the creation of an international system capable of securing the acquiescence of weaker states and classes, by claiming to represent universal interests. Such an achievement depended on a coherent fit between the three basic forces of any structure of power: material capabilities, ideas and institutions; emblematically, in the case of the *pax Britannica*—the command of sea power, the liberal ideology of free trade, and the regulative functions of the City of London.[1] Such a configuration always

---

1   'Social Forces, States and World Orders: Beyond International Relations Theory', *Millennium*, 1982, No. 2, p. 1240: his theoretical manifesto.

rested on social forces located in particular relations of production. Once these altered, the effects would ricochet through the whole system. Classically, as Carr had shown, with the arrival of heavy industry in Europe, an industrial working class had emerged whose demands for welfare led to pressures for protection that intensified inter-state rivalries, which in exploding with the First World War finished off British hegemony. Those states were most powerful which underwent a deep socio-economic revolution and worked out its full consequences, and by joining 'an ideological and inter-subjective element to the brute power relationship' gained a hegemony exceeding any mere imperialism. Such was the position enjoyed by the United States after the Second World War.

Though neither ever cited the other, the match between Cox's and Arrighi's formulations was thus very close. But it was not complete. Partly this was a function of differences of background and audience. However radical in outlook, Cox was a product of his service: the ILO was not the Gruppo Gramsci, and his style in the academy was more conventional. While distinguishing between 'problem-solving' and 'critical' theory, he was not ill at ease with the former, his work appearing in collections or journals alongside those concerned to prop up the structures he criticised, and addressed in the first instance to the professional international relations community, rather than to any wider political audience of the left. On the other hand, in exposition he was more expressly and systematically Gramscian than Arrighi.[2] The more significant differences, however, lay elsewhere. Each was strong where the other was less so. In Cox there is no long-range theory of financialisation,

---

2   See 'Gramsci, Hegemony and International Relations: An Essay in Method', *Millennium* 1983, No. 2, pp. 162–75: paper originally presented to the American Political Science Association in 1981.

and no dialectic of territorialism and capitalism: national states lack historical exploration or weight in his writing. Classes, on the other hand, figure in greater depth and nuance—Cox made much more use of Gramsci's notion of a historical bloc—and international norms and institutions feature more prominently as disciplinary elements of a hegemonic system. Crucially, in the contemporary world, where production was becoming increasingly transnational in structure, a corresponding managerial class was emerging at the apex of the system, and the hegemonic order was interweaving social forces across state boundaries into new hierarchical patterns. Cox considered with care not only the range of dominant and subordinate groups but differing types of production around the world,[3] as they presented themselves in the last years of Reagan's mandate, over a decade after the onset of the long downturn in the early seventies.

Where in these new circumstances did American hegemony stand? At the time, Cox concluded, as Arrighi would do, that amid continuing crisis and symptoms of disorder, it was declining into mere dominance, a judgment he was to alter over the succeeding years. But the influence of his work did not always lead in the same direction. Distinctive of the 'neo-Gramscian' schools directly or indirectly inspired by it would be the emphasis in Cox's thinking on transnational class blocs and their articulation with the hegemon. In this intellectual tradition, the most developed analysis of the constellation of global forces in

---

3   In *Production, Power and World Order*, Cox distinguished twelve differ-
    ent 'modes of social relations' in the late twentieth century: subsistence,
    peasant-lord, primitive labour market, household, self-employment,
    enterprise labour market, bipartism, enterprise corporatism, tripartism,
    state corporatism, communal, state planning: pp. 32–103. Work for the
    ILO left its mark on this typology, but in spirit it was closer to Arrighi's
    early writing on Rhodesia and Calabria than to his later work.

the wake of the financial crisis of 2008–2009 arrived at a different verdict. In an essay produced in Britain situating itself in a line from Cox, Richard Saull would offer a striking counter-interpretation of the time. *Contra* Arrighi, US hegemony was not in any terminal decline.[4] Financialisation had generated a more crisis-ridden form of capitalism, but when the crash of 2008 came, America and its partners in the G-7 had shown their capacity to cooperate in responding to it. To date there was no evidence of a basic shift in economic power away from the US. China was not a contender for effecting one, since its model of growth still depended on exports to the US, tethering Beijing to subordinate relations with Washington. Efforts to move towards a model based on domestic consumption required further liberalisation of the Chinese economy, risking not only erosion of the power of the CCP, but capital flight and rising social tensions. The *pax Americana* was in no real danger from that quarter. Nor from any traditional inter-state challenge. For its hegemonic system was secured not primarily by coercive or authoritarian means, but by embedding its inequitable pattern of social power in the domestic economic arrangements of other states, and the ideological, cultural and political norms associated with these.

In the post-war era, American predominance had forged a historical bloc that incorporated the working class of the West around Fordist patterns of mass production and rising consumption, topped up with anti-communist ideology. Over time that had been undermined by the emergence of new forms of production and social relations at the micro-level of firms, rather than by any deliberate strategy on the part of other states.

---

4   'Rethinking Hegemony: Uneven Development, Historical Blocs and the World Economic Crisis', *International Studies Quarterly*, June 2012, pp. 323–38.

But the breakdown of the organic formula of *les trente glorieuses* did not spell a decline of US hegemony, because by the eighties another historical bloc had come into being, incorporating much more of the developing world into the arrangements of neoliberalism, drawing ever wider regions of the earth and layers of the world's population into capitalist relations of production. In the West, organised labour was expelled from this historical bloc by a crackdown on unions and outsourcing of jobs, but workers were integrated into it with a new division of labour, easy credit, naturalisation of debt, and cheaper goods from East Asia. In East Asia too, the neoliberal dispensation of individualised consumption and freedom of choice, laced with an admixture of nationalism, was not unattractive to elements of the working class.

Most significant, however, was the incorporation of the new middle classes of Brazil, India and China into an emergent transnational bloc of neo-liberal stamp. In Brazil financialisation, property speculation, and a mania for luxury goods, in India corporate takeover of global brands and psychic alignment with Washington, were hallmarks of this stratum. In all three countries the same kind of import and absorption of production processes, consumption patterns and technological innovations from the US that had shaped the Fordist era in Western Europe and Japan was under way. Unlike Western Europe and Japan, however, China, India and Brazil had preserved their autonomy as states from the geopolitical grip of the US, and large parts of their societies were far from integrated into the neoliberal world order, creating many domestic tensions, especially in China. The complex hierarchical system of American hegemony did not possess universal coverage. But it was stable enough.

II

The strength of this diagnostic lay, as with Cox's vision at large, in its sense of the transnational—as distinct from international or national—dimensions of the hegemony of the civilisation of capital in the twenty-first century, and their condensation in the ideological forms of neoliberalism: 'disciplinary' or 'compensatory' as the context required, in the telling formula of another theorist of the same school.[5] Less developed is the articulation between these three planes, the transnational tending to blur the contours of the other two, as if encompassing them, at the cost of obscuring their specificity: each endowed with coercive powers which the transnational, by Weberian definition, does not possess. That such a misstep was not necessary would be shown by a Chinese thinker whose work on his country registers not a few of the processes Saull describes. For Wang Hui, it is a depoliticisation of politics that is the mark of the current age: that is, the cancellation of any popular agency able to carry or fight for an alternative to a status quo that simulates representative forms the better to empty them of division or conflict. Such politics is depoliticised, but it is not de-ideologised. On the contrary, it is ideological through and through. It is enough to consider the first of the three planes of hegemony analysed by Wang Hui—the national level, and its ideological crystallisation in the homelands of the neoliberalism that swept the world over the succeeding decades, the Britain of Thatcher and the United

---

5   Stephen Gill, 'A Neo-Gramscian Approach to European Integration', in Alan Cafruny and Magnus Ryder (eds), *A Ruined Fortress? Neoliberal Hegemony and Transformation in Europe*, Lanham 2003, pp. 65–7. Saull's other principal reference, Gill joined Cox in Toronto after emigrating from Thatcherite England. Unlike Saull, he would suggest that the US now enjoyed, at best, 'supremacy' in a 'post-hegemonic world': *Power and Resistance in the New World Order*, New York 2003, pp. 118–20, 140–1, 180.

States of Reagan. It was Thatcher who coined the most famous slogan of neoliberalism, capturing the essence of depoliticised politics—TINA: There is No Alternative. No alternative, that is, to the rule of deregulated financial markets: the reign of capital as the reign of freedom. But this was far from the only ideological equipment of the Thatcher and Reagan regimes. In itself too dry, too blunt, and in its own way too truthful to the realities of the time, it always required a supplement covering and cushioning it. In Britain, this was supplied by a combination of nationalism and family values, as Thatcher called them; in the United States, the supplement was nationalism and religion. Such ideological duality is the typical formula of a hegemony at national level. Historically, China provided one of the earliest and the most long-lasting of all such combinations. There contemporaries needed only to think of the centuries of state power that, according to the well-known formula *ru biao, fa li* were, as the historian He Bingdi put it, ornamentally Confucian and functionally Legalist—not to speak of its possible modern variations.

What of the third component of hegemony in the depoliticised universe Wang Hui described—the transnational or global component, operative at neither state nor inter-state levels, but cutting across all frontiers at cultural and societal levels? As he noted: 'Hegemony relates not only to national or international relations, but is intimately connected to transnational and supra-national capitalism; it must also be analysed within the sphere of globalised market relations'. What was its substance there? 'The most direct expressions of the market-ideological apparatus are the media, advertising, the "world of shopping", and so forth. These mechanisms are not only commercial, but ideological. Their greatest power lies in their appeal to "common sense", ordinary needs which turn people into consumers, voluntarily following market logic in their daily lives.'[6]

Here consumerism is identified as a linchpin of the global hegemony of capital. But at this level too, the structure of hegemony today is dual. Consumption—certainly: a terrain of ideological capture in one domain of daily life. But capitalism is at its base a system of production, and it is in work as well as leisure that its hegemony is reproduced in the 'dull compulsion of alienated labour', as Marx called it, that relentlessly adapts its subjects to existing social relations, deadening their energies and abilities to imagine any other and better order of the world. It is this dual existential structure, in the interlocking universe of production and consumption—the one a compensation, half-real and half-illusory, for the other—that lies at the base of the transnational forms of hegemony of neo-Gramscian concern.

---

6 'Depoliticized Politics, from East to West', *New Left Review* 41, September–October 2006, p. 42.

11

ENDURING OR EBBING

These were critics of America's role in the world after the end of the Cold War. How should patriots conceive it? On the eve of US triumph over the USSR, Nye had dismissed the *pax Americana* as a myth and talk of hegemony as a confusion. The correct term for the contribution of the United States to the international community, as Kindleberger had indicated, was leadership. But once America was installed as sole superpower, could that bracing locution, free from any suspicion of force, still cover its new position? There were more antiseptic alternatives, lacking its moral afflatus, available: primacy or unipolarity, favoured by some. But such usages was soon overwhelmed by the proliferation of books and torrent of articles in which, unabashed by Nye's strictures, hegemony became common currency in the nineties. In the ranks of mainstream thinkers, provided they were not at the time functionaries of one administration or the other, an adjustment had to come. Ten years on from Nye's *Bound to Lead*, John Ikenberry traced a symptomatic equivocation. *After Victory* (2001) looked back at the great achievements of the US in constructing a new international order after the Second World War, integrating Germany and Japan into an economic and security system under its leadership. That had assured the peace and prosperity of the West. Now America was set fair to repeat the feat in handling the defeated Soviet bloc. Had it ever been, was it now, a hegemon? That, it would seem at first, must be a misnomer. Hegemonic orders were hierarchical, and whether openly coercive or relatively more benign, were 'essentially based on unchecked power'—quite unlike a 'constitutional order', where 'agreed-upon legal and political institutions operate to allocate rights and limit power', taming power to 'make it less consequential'.[1] The post-war settlement was essentially constitutional, the United States binding itself to a set of restraints limiting the returns to its asymmetrical power in the comity of democracies. Yet mention of hegemony, however inconsistent with the contrast initially made between the two, could not altogether be banished. American hegemony, it had to be conceded, there was after all. But it was not only 'reluctant', but singularly 'open and penetrated', allowing other states to find their voice within the prosperity and peace it brought.[2] Still, this remained a constitutional order, one of whose foundations, NATO—basically 'a defensive aggregation of power'—had now happily been enlarged to the east. Since all its members were pluralistic democracies, the Foreign Minister of Russia could justly observe that this 'practically rules out the pursuance of an aggressive foreign policy'.[3]

Returning to the charge a year later, Ikenberry was more candidly affirmative. He now explained that there was no contradiction between a constitutional and a hegemonic order, indeed that the first was the most helpful lubricant of the second. For 'a constitutional settlement conserves hegemonic power', by at once locking in arrangements favourable to it, and

---

1   *After Victory: Institutions, Strategic Restraint, and the Rebuilding of Order after Major Wars*, Princeton 2001, pp. 27–9.
2   *After Victory*, pp. 53 ff., 200–5.
3   *After Victory*, p. 19: Andrei Kozyrev *dixit*.

reducing the costs of enforcing order that would otherwise fall to it. The institutions and relations such a hegemony fostered around itself then inevitably yielded increasing returns to it. 'A good analogy is computer software, where a software provider like Microsoft, after gaining an initial market advantage, encourages the proliferation of software applications and programs based on Microsoft's operating language. This in turn creates a huge complex of providers and users who are heavily dependent on the Microsoft format' and an 'increasingly dense set of commitments to Microsoft' based on 'the growing reality that changing to another format would be more costly, even if it were more efficient.'

So too any major shifts in the basic organisation of—what could now straightforwardly be called—'the American hegemonic order' would be 'increasingly costly to a widening array of individuals and groups who make up the order. More and more people have a stake in the system, even if they have no particular loyalty or affinity to the United States and even if they might really prefer a different order', since 'more and more people would have their lives disrupted if the system were to be radically changed'. In that sense 'the American post-war order is stable and growing'.[4] This was certainly a satisfactory outcome for the United States. But it also answered to more general requirements of the time. American power was acceptable to the rest of the world because 'the United States "project" is congruent with the deeper forces of modernisation'.[5]

---

4   'Democracy, Institutions and American Restraint', in John Ikenberry (ed.), *America Unrivalled: The Future of the Balance of Power*, Ithaca 2002, p. 234–5.
5   'Conclusion', *America Unrivalled*: not only the self-restraint of the United States, but 'the deep congruence between the internal American system—and its civic and multicultural identity—and the long-term project of modernity also gives the unipolar order its robustness': pp. 296, 310.

So too for other contributors to the same volume. Denial of American hegemony no longer made sense; what it called for was approval. 'My emphasis on hegemony is not meant as a radical critique', one writer still felt it necessary to explain. For in fact 'US hegemony is peculiarly benign. Not only does it allow smaller countries relatively more influence over the hegemon, but it also promotes human flourishing—freedom and prosperity—better than any alternative yet tried.'[6] It was true, another observed, that its sway was not entire: the two largest countries in Asia lay outside the US security system. So the challenge lay ahead of 'completing hegemony', by integrating China and India into the American order without alienating Japan. That would not be easy. But the historic resentments and mutual suspicions in the region, setting one state against another, were a reason for each to seek a special relationship with the US, creating conditions for success in the task. Admittedly, 'no-one loves a global hegemon. But US hegemony is sufficiently benign to be at least tolerable—even to states with great power aspirations of their own.'[7]

Such was the effective consensus at the turn of the millennium. Leadership might have edged towards hegemony, to which snipers had at times given a negative connotation, but though it had a stronger ring of authority, the newfangled term implied, no less than the old, benefits freely conferred and guidance willingly accepted, stray malcontents apart. From late 2001 onwards, however, this semantic equilibrium had to withstand the shock of 9/11, the invasion of Afghanistan, the war on Iraq and all that followed. The result was a potential further shift.

6   John M. Owen IV, 'Transnational Liberalism and American Primacy: or, Benignity is in the Eye of the Beholder', *America Unrivalled*, pp. 241–2.
7   Michael Mastanduno, 'Incomplete Hegemony and Security Order in the Asia-Pacific', *America Unrivalled*, pp. 203, 209–10.

Was hegemony really distinguishable from empire? That, confessed one classical historian, had already been a question in Ancient Greece, where it could not be denied that empire was the 'evil twin' of hegemony.[8] Soon another large literature sprang up, embracing, attacking or denying the imperial operations or ambitions of the United States around the world.[9]

Adjusting to new circumstances, a decade later Ikenberry swapped the language of a constitution for that of a bargain. 'What is distinctive about hegemonic order is that it is a bargained order in which the lead state provides services and frameworks of cooperation. In return, it invites participation and compliance by weaker and secondary states'. American hegemony was definitionally liberal, based on shared rules and reciprocity of gains: 'the US shapes and dominates the international order while guaranteeing a flow of benefits to other governments that earns their acquiescence. In contrast to empire, this negotiated order depends on agreements regarding the rules of the system between the leading state and everyone else'. True, it included patron-client relations with peripheral states that were more asymmetrical in character, and 'other mechanisms of order—balance and command—also lurk at the edges of the liberal international order'.[10] But the difference of principle and reality held good. There had been no American empire.

Did the foreign policy of the Republican administration after 2001 alter this? Seeking to 'overhaul the global security

8 Wickersham, *Hegemony and Greek Historians*, p. 23.
9 For references as of 2009, see Paul K. Macdonald, 'Those who forget historiography are doomed to republish it: empire, imperialism and contemporary debates about American power', *Review of International Studies*, January 2009, pp. 45–67, dividing the field into imperial enthusiasts, imperial critics and imperial sceptics.
10 *The Liberal Leviathan: The Origins, Crisis and Transformation of the American World Order*, Princeton 2011, pp. 70, 66.

system', it had 'embraced the logic of a post-Westphalian world and offered a new hegemonic bargain with the world', but in doing so had unfortunately placed the US above the rules it imposed on others, making the bargain less palatable to them. In consequence, other countries had tended to 'under-supply cooperation', and in a brief lapsus of dismay, Ikenberry could exclaim that 'this is, in effect, empire'. No sooner said than suppressed. What Bush had made of unipolar American power after 9/11 was rather an 'illiberal hegemony'—the inconspicuous prefix sufficient to hold the line between the two, and allow for recovery of the 'authority and respect' the country had traditionally enjoyed, in recommitment to the 'grand strategy of liberal order building'.[11]

If this was a case of the need to defend an ideological investment already long made, more significant were two substantial interventions from historians, each conservative in outlook, but antipodal in temperament. In his *Colossus* (2004), Niall Ferguson, while noting that more level-headed spirits had recently been rallying to the term, argued that America was still, officially speaking, an empire in denial. The most popular word for describing its place in the world had become hegemony, but the distinction between the two descriptions rested on a definition of empire as direct political rule, formally declared as such, over foreign territories, which had long been superseded by a more sophisticated understanding of the variety of forms in which imperial power could be exercised; not to speak of

---

11 *The Liberal Leviathan*, pp. 276, 270, 360. The chapter dealing with Republican foreign policy is entitled 'The Great Transformation and the Failure of Illiberal Hegemony'. Three years later, Ikenberry was hailing return to the 'great American postwar global best practice' under a Democratic presidency, and the 'full spectrum internationalism' of its incumbent, with unbounded enthusiasm: 'Obama's Pragmatic Internationalism', *The American Interest*, 8 April 2014.

the range of political regimes—from Augustan Rome through Victorian Britain to Nazi Germany and now the Land of the Free—that could deploy such power, of which Ferguson offered a grid. 'With a broader and more sophisticated definition of empire', he observed. 'it seems possible to dispense altogether with the term *hegemony*.'[12] As to value judgments, he made no secret of his own: 'I am fundamentally in favour of empire.' But while standing foursquare behind his adoptive country's pursuit of it, Ferguson was no cheerleader. The liberal empire of the United States, an enterprise at once of national self-interest and global altruism, was the best hope of the developed world and, contrary to its critics, the aims of its invasion of Iraq were both laudable and attainable. But there was good reason to fear that the nation would not be up to its destiny. For unlike imperial Britain, few among its citizens were willing to spend their lives monitoring or administering distant lands; its voters were short-winded; its soldiers were over-protected; and—most decisively—its fiscal future was in mortmain to entitlements it could not meet. Disquietingly, 'the global power of the United States today—impressive though it is to behold—rests on much weaker foundations than is commonly supposed'. For Americans 'would rather consume than conquer. They would rather build shopping malls than nations. They crave for themselves protracted old age and dread, even for other Americans who have volunteered for military service, untimely death in battle.'[13] Sadly, the danger to the American empire came not from rivals without, but from 'the absence of a will to power' within.

The outstanding expression of the antithetical standpoint came from Paul Schroeder, historian of international politics

---

12 *Colossus: The Rise and Fall of the American Empire,* New York 2004, p. 12.
13 *Colossus,* pp. 24, 28–9.

in Europe from the Peace of Paris in 1763 to the outbreak of
the Great War in 1914. Alone among scholars in the US, he
had warned within weeks of 9/11—before even the invasion
of Afghanistan, let alone Iraq—of the dangers of US military
intervention in a region where it did not historically belong,
predicting that easy initial success was likely to bring ultimate
disaster,[14] and over the next six years, published a series of
excoriating critiques of the war to overthrow the Baath regime,
in analytic force unique in the literature of the time. A few days
before American troops entered Baghdad, when the triumph of
Operation Iraqi Freedom was already object of celebration in
the US media, Schroeder wrote an essay entitled 'The Mirage of
Empire versus the Promise of Hegemony', that remains the most
systematic counterposition of the two conceptions ever made.
Empire was political control over foreigners, more often informal than direct, but final authority resting with the imperial
state. Hegemony, by contrast was 'acknowledged leadership and
superior influence by one power within a community of units
not a single authority'. Empires functioned to rule, hegemonies
to manage. The decisions of the former were imperative, of
the latter merely indispensable. Crucially, hegemony was fully
compatible with the modern international system composed of
autonomous states, juridically equal in status, however unequal
in power, whereas empire was not.[15]

Attempts at empire invariably bred chaos and war, where
hegemonies were often either architects or conditions of peace
and stability, their absence indeed leading to a breakdown in
international order. Schroeder conceded that 'this distinction

---

14 'The Risks of Victory', *The National Interest*, Winter 2001–2002, pp. 22–36.
15 'The Mirage of Empire versus the Promise of Hegemony', *Systems, Stability
and Statecraft: Essays on the International History of Modern Europe*, New
York 2004, pp. 298–9; recalling and commending Stadelmann's conception
of hegemony as 'guided balance': p. 363.

like most such distinctions in social and intellectual life is not airtight, but one of degree, like the difference between warm, hot, and boiling'. It was also true that hegemonic powers could become empires and were regularly tempted to do so. But that did not cancel the distinction. From the sixteenth to the twentieth centuries, it could be illustrated in two opposite sets of rulers—Charles V, Philip II, Ferdinand II, Louis XIV, Charles XII, Napoleon, Hitler and Stalin on one side; Ferdinand I, Richelieu and Mazarin, Leopold I, Fleury, the victors of 1815, Bismarck, and 'the most obvious and impressive example', the US after 1945, on the other. Disastrously, with the conquest and occupation of Iraq, America was now taking the road to empire, as if it could replicate the British takeover of Egypt in the late nineteenth century, when none of the historical conditions that had made that possible any longer existed. In the twenty-first century, Victorian imperialism could not be revived.

No stronger argument for separating hegemony from empire has yet been, or is likely to be, made. Yet even this attempt cannot escape the aporia of so many others. How could empire be incompatible with a modern state system going back to the sixteenth century, when every major European state, and not a few minor ones, had acquired an empire by 1914? Were the two leading powers at the Vienna Congress, each in possession of territories conquered by force, not indivisibly imperial and hegemonic in Restoration Europe? Did the Mexican War of 1846–48 occur in some universe outside the international system? Does the enormous increase in the disparities of power within the hierarchy of the states of the late twentieth and twenty-first century—far greater than in the eighteenth or nineteenth centuries—have no implications for the exercise of imperial authority, postmodern-style? How much autonomy do states possess that can be subjected to overwhelming economic pressure, political and cultural penetration, military basing and more, reducing them to client status, or less, with every respect for their nominal sovereignty? The twins are not enemies; they cohabit comfortably enough.

II

The word arrived in the United States from Europe as a term of international politics, and there in common parlance it remained such. What has become of that usage in the continent that gave rise to it, and is taken by every reputable authority as the region *par excellence* freely accepting and benefitting from American hegemony—often indeed characterised, in the formula of a grateful if not entirely tactful Norwegian, as an 'empire by invitation'? Britain, with the largest former empire, and closest relationship to the US, developed under the *pax Americana* the most substantial tradition of thinking about international relations: a distinctive 'English School', at its best—in the work of its two most original minds, Martin Wight and Hedley Bull—of significantly greater historical and intellectual depth than the run of IR as a discipline in the US.[16] In the first generation of this school, Carr was an influence that could not be escaped, however distant its political outlook—by no means uniform—was from him. The trademark of the school, though its least coherent

---

16 Wight, the doyen of the School, combined crystalline analysis and breadth of culture—his *Power Politics* (1946) and posthumous *International Theory: the Three Traditions* (1991) remain classics—with apocalyptic religion, welcoming the outbreak of the Second War as divine judgment on humanity for its apostasy, and identifying figures of the Anti-Christ all the way from the emperor Julian to Hitler, 'the final concentration of Satanic evil' before the Second Coming: Ian Hall, *The International Thought of Martin Wight*, New York 2006, pp. 33–7. In later years, though still believing a nuclear war was preferable to a world state, he settled down to a more sedate defence of Western values.

notion, was the idea that there had emerged in Europe from the early modern epoch onwards not merely an inter-state system, but an 'international society' of states sharing common interests and values, and bound by common rules and procedures, constituting a normative universe overarching them, propitious to compromise and peace between them. For Carr this was a pious fiction. No such thing as an international society existed, merely an 'open club without substantive rules'. The work of the English School, as of its transatlantic counterparts, was little more than a study of 'how to run the world from a position of strength'.[17] As for the ethical pretensions of the society it imagined, he remarked drily, 'power always creates a morality convenient to itself'.

This was to underestimate his own impact on what he scorned. Though Wight, after extraordinarily gifted beginnings, eventually subsided into the truisms of Atlantic self-congratulation, this was never true of Bull, a level-headed Australian who not only argued that international society, as he conceived it, was always in tension with a state of war as a Hobbesian default position of the inter-state system, as well as with political forces cutting across states borders, but itself rested on a series of 'institutions'—in the strained vocabulary of the school—that included not only a hierarchy of states dominated by the Great Powers but war itself, along with more reassuring landmarks like diplomacy, international law, and the balance of power. An international society of this kind could come in two versions, minimal or maximal—a 'pluralist' community of states respecting each other's sovereignty, and a 'solidarist' one imposing common norms within each state, enforced by a supranational authority or civil society. Order was the governing objective of the first, justice of the second. Bull was in no doubt that the

---

17 Letter to Stanley Hoffman, 30 September 1977: Jonathan Haslam, *The Vices of Integrity: E. H. Carr, 1892–1982*, London-New York 1999, pp. 252–3.

former was both more realistic and less open to abuse than the latter.

The second generation of the school, in the epoch of the Non-Proliferation Treaty, the Responsibility to Protect, Humanitarian Intervention, the War on Terror and the like, reversed this preference. Pluralism was not enough. Solidarism required less circumspection with sovereignty, more sense of *le droit d'ingérence* of the 'international community', as it could now—a refreshing development—officially be called. What place was there in this new, essentially progressive constellation for hegemony? Bull had certainly not regarded it as one of the pillar institutions of international society. 'Where a great power exercises hegemony over the lesser powers', he observed, 'there is resort to force and the threat of force', even if this was occasional and reluctant rather than uninhibited and habitual, other instruments for imposing its will being available. Hegemony was 'imperialism with good manners'.[18]

This was altogether too blunt for the next levy. There was, however, an alternative construction in the English School, proposed by the former diplomat Adam Watson, which gave much ampler scope to hegemony, within a taxonomy of state systems stretching back to the dawn of civilisation in Mesopotamia—a conceptual arc running from empire at one end, through dominion and suzerainty, to hegemony and independent states at the other end. Historically, if the arc was regarded as a pendulum, there was a gravitational pull away from both empire and independence towards the centre, where hegemony was virtually ubiquitous if there existed a multiplicity of formally independent but factually unequal states.[19] As a form it should be viewed

---

18 *The Anarchical Society: A Study of Order in World Politics*, Basingstoke 1977, p. 209.

19 *The Evolution of International Society: A Comparative Analysis*, London

dispassionately, not pejoratively. Hegemony, although naturally requiring military force, did not operate through a dictatorial fiat: it involved dialogue and a sense of mutual expediency. On the other hand, whereas Watson had originally maintained hegemons controlled only the external relations of subordinate states, he eventually concluded that hegemonic pressures quickly extended to their internal affairs, potentially affecting everything from their economic and political systems to their religious orientation or social structure.[20]

This was a more understanding vision of hegemony, but the Olympian scale of the retrospect of which it formed an element also distanced it from issues of urgent concern to later members of the English School. 'International society', as after all Watson himself had noted, was constitutionally 'anti-hegemonial'. Did not US preponderance risk forestalling the moral consensus on which it depended? For how could international society retain its legitimacy if one state was able routinely to impose its will on others? Writing in 2005, Ian Clark—holder of the chair Carr once occupied, and the most prolific of his cohort—worried that a new US unilateralism was threatening 'prevailing notions of constitutionality'. The problem was not American hegemony as such, but the lack so far of a 'satisfactory *principle of hegemony*' that could render it palatable to a sufficiently wide number of

---

1992, pp. 13–16, 314. Watson, whose postings included wartime Romania and Egypt, five years in post-war Moscow, duties in psychological warfare, head of the Africa desk after Suez, with a final assignment as ambassador to Cuba in the sixties, had the widest historical range of the English School: a figure unthinkable in today's Foreign Office.

20 'I formerly thought of hegemony as that area of the spectrum between multiple absolute independences and a single world government that allows dominant powers to influence the external policies of other states, but not or only marginally their domestic policies. Now I realise how much the hegemony of the West and especially the United States also aims to modify the internal behaviour of other states and communities': *Hegemony and History*, London 2007, pp. 80, 104.

states, securing 'moral acceptance of an idea of hegemony'. If this could be found, international society could reach an accommodation with US power. Its legitimacy had been wounded by the invasion of Iraq, but legitimacy was not the same as legality, which was only one consideration for it. Rather, of its nature legitimacy was 'politically dynamic', adjusting to circumstances. A hopeful sign was the retroactive UN resolution endorsing the occupation of Iraq, a 'blessing of critical importance to future outcomes'.[21]

In the task of legitimising US hegemony, the English School had a special responsibility. Regrettably, it had in the past seemed 'much more committed to the prevention of hegemony than with exploring consensual compliance with it'. Yet what had always animated it as a project was 'the management of order in a world of power differentials', and if it had assumed an international society in which there were a number of great powers, would it not be contrary to the spirit of the school to abandon its mission when there was just one? After *Legitimacy in International Society* came its requisite complement, *Hegemony in International Society*, starting with the Congress of Vienna and extending to Obama. Its conclusions? There was a tension between two principles of international order, the near-universal acceptance of the need for great powers to play a leading role in its management, and the need for there to be some balance between them so their power was not abused. How was the first to be preserved in the absence of the second? Here the English School could make itself 'relevant to contemporary conditions', by supplying the 'missing piece in the architecture' of its thought, without which it 'found itself at dead end'. The solution was for international society to 'socialise' hegemony, by 'adopting it as an institution of its own making'—hegemony

21 *Legitimacy in International Society*, Oxford 2005, pp. 216, 242, 253–4, 256.

becoming an 'institutionalised practice of special rights and responsibilities conferred by international society or a constituency within it, on a state (or states) with the resources to lead'.[22] America did not yet enjoy this true hegemony, though Obama showed a better understanding of it. But there the key to a stable and orderly world must lie.

'A constituency within it' … Why fuss about its extent? Since Bull, the school of which he was a founder has descended into apologetics, in pursuit of relevance; Clark, more critical in outlook in his earlier work, is not an isolated nor an extreme case.[23] The populariser of the school, Barry Buzan, is less varnished, steering clear even of this elevating version of hegemony for the safer Nye-style euphemisms of leadership. 'There can be no question that the US has been an astoundingly successful and constructive international leader over the last half century and that there are no candidates around that look capable of doing the job equally well or better'—indeed, whatever its occasional failings, US leadership in that time has had a 'broadly benign effect on the development of international society unprecedented in the annals of history'. Bush had endangered this leadership, but French criticisms of it should be 'relentlessly opposed'.[24] Only friends like Britain could

22 *Hegemony in International Society*, Oxford 2011, pp. 4, 36, 49, 56, 241.

23 The intellectual curve of Clark's oeuvre from the clear- to the misty-eyed— from *The Hierarchy of States* (1989), *Globalization and Fragmentation* (1997) and *The Post-Cold War Order* (2001), to *Legitimacy in International Society* (2005), *International Legitimacy and World Society* (2007), and *Hegemony in International Society* (2011)—is pronounced.

24 *The United States and the Great Powers: World Politics in the Twenty-First Century,* Cambridge 2004, pp. 188, 193–4. By origin, Buzan is a Canadian. He prefaces his declaration of faith in the United States with the proviso, 'unless one is entirely opposed to capitalism', which he elsewhere pronounces 'the only game in town'—though preferring to speak of 'the market': *Introduction to the English School of International Relations: the Societal Approach*, Cambridge 2014, p. 138.

influence American beliefs about the way their country might be perceived abroad, and help it back to the course it had followed so superbly in the past: a tradition once marked by a notable independence of mind shrinking to the trite abasements of the Special Relationship. In two memorable sentences, Bull marked the difference between his outlook and most of those who came after him, and wrote their epitaph. At the outset of his major work, he remarked: 'inquiry has its own morality, and is necessarily subversive of political institutions and movements of all kinds, good as well as bad', and at its ending: 'The search for conclusions that can be presented as "solutions" or "practical advice" is a corrupting element in the contemporary study of world politics'.[25]

25 *The Anarchical Society*, pp. xxxvii, 308.

12

ASPIRING

If the late contortions of 'international society' in Britain—in Clark's words, nurturing the plant of hegemony in theoretical soil apparently inhospitable to it—could be read as intellectual symptoms of the attempt by an empire of the past to dignify its role as adjutant to the empire of the present, a movement in the opposite direction, vindicating the rise of a power of the future, could be seen in Europe. There in 2012, in Germany's leading journal of ideas, the jurist Christoph Schönberger proclaimed his country's arrival as hegemon of the European Union.[1] This was not hegemony in its Anglophone meaning, as predominance in an inter-state system, let alone its vulgar anti-imperialist usage in Gramsci (Vacca would have been startled), but in the strict sense expounded by Triepel: leadership within a federation, as in the role of Athens in the Delian League, Holland in the United Provinces and Prussia in the Second Reich. The EU was a federation composed of over two dozen states of vastly differing size and significance, each with formally equal rights of membership, whose complex machinery in Brussels lacked any transparent connexion with the domestic publics of the

---

1 'Hegemon wider Willen. Zur Stellung Deutschlands in der Europäische Union', *Merkur* January 2012, pp. 1–8.

continent, and indeed had to be sound-proofed against them if it was to run smoothly. Coherence and direction in this unwieldy structure could only come from a state unmistakably larger and stronger than all others, as Prussia had been in the Second Reich of Bismarck's creation.

Germany was now that power, and Germans must shed the provincial introversion of a recent past, and come to terms with a role they could no longer avoid. In the Federal Republic, a meddlesome parliament and obstructive constitutional court, each narrowing the scope for bold executive action, were local difficulties. So too was an idealised yearning for democracy typical of peoples with a recent undemocratic past, uncomfortable with the opaque bureaucracy of the Commission and its maze of technocratic committees—the kind of longing voiced by Habermas, with his dreams of a supranational democracy electing a government answerable to a pan-European electorate. Notions of this kind were political science fiction. The only feasible reality was a federation of states, equal in theory, hierarchical in practice, led by a hegemonic Germany. France, with its unreformed economy and faded accoutrements of prestige—nuclear weapons and a seat in the Security Council—would have to adjust to a position like much that of Bavaria under Bismarck: compensated for loss of power with soothing gestures and side payments. There was no arrogance in predicting this configuration. Germany was becoming a hegemon against its own will, and such hegemony would be more a burden than a privilege. It was the country's fate.

Warned by Helmut Schmidt that this message was an indiscretion that could harm German interests, Schönberger was at pains to dispel any misunderstanding.[2] In speaking of hegemony, he was not in any way using the term as it was often

---

2   'Nochmals: die Deutsche Hegemonie', *Merkur* January 2013, pp. 25–33.

loosely applied to great power politics. Triepel had criticised that confusion, restricting the term to federal (as distinct from international) structures of power, and made it clear that all it involved was a 'determining influence'. Germany, moreover, had no overwhelming margin of power in Europe, less than Prussia had enjoyed in the Second Reich. So there was nothing to be alarmed about. True, it was unlikely to be much loved; hegemons rarely were. But it would be respected as such, provided it showed itself able to manage the affairs of the Union in a disinterested spirit. A certain narrowness of economic outlook might stand in the way of that. It would be wise not to insist too much that its partners adopt its economic culture, the product of a particular past, or imply they could all reproduce its export model, which was not possible. But as against such blinkers, the political culture of the country was ideally suited to its role as hegemon of the Union, since Germany itself was a federation of some complexity, whose political elites had long experience of the kind of pragmatic bargaining and mutual adjustment that was the essence of EU management.

This modestly reassuring tone did not survive the book-length sequel on the country's position in Europe published two years later by Herfried Münkler, holder of the chair for Political Theory at the Humboldt University in Berlin, and Germany's most prominent exponent of a comparative geopolitics. Best-known for a world-historical study of empires vindicating their role in imposing order on a vacuum of power around them—tribal or other forms of anarchy in the past, weak or failed states in more recent times—Münkler had saluted America's interventions in the Balkans and the Middle East, not to speak of the War on Terror, as the latest enterprise in this line of succession. Europe, he had urged, should develop a comparable imperial politics of its own, capable of policing its periphery in analogous style, in a loyal parallelism with the US.[3] As of 2006, Germany had started to act as a more self-confident 'medium power', dispatching its troops abroad in the common interest. But it still relied too much on its economic prowess for its national self-assertion. It needed to diversify its portfolio of power.

A decade later, Germany could be assigned an altogether greater role. *Macht in der Mitte* (2015) lays out the reasons why the Bundesrepublik has at last achieved the position in Europe at which previous regimes stumbled. 'We are the Hegemon', Münkler now announced.[4] For not only was Germany the largest economy and most populous nation in the Union, it set the standard for social cohesion and political competence. Unlike France, it had carried out with Agenda 2010 a thorough-going reform of its labour market and welfare entitlements, leaving its one-time partner in EU management far behind in pace of growth and export performance. Unlike Italy, where despite decades of futile expenditures, the Mezzogiorno was still a backward fetter on the North, it had successfully raised its impoverished and uncompetitive East towards Western levels of efficiency and prosperity. Unlike every other major country of Europe—France, Italy, Spain, Britain—its citizens had so far shown themselves proof against populism of any kind, right or left, stabilising their neighbours with a unique spectacle of political responsibility. Certainly, there should be no complacency, since symptoms of the same disorder were starting to appear in Germany itself, with the *Alternative für Deutschland*. But these only made more inevitable a continuance of the collaboration between the CDU and SPD in occupation of the middle ground

---

3   *Imperien*, Berlin 2006, pp. 245–54. For a trenchant analysis of this work, see Benno Teschke, 'Imperial Doxa from the Berlin Republic', *New Left Review* 40, July–August 2006, pp. 128–40.

4   'Wir sind der Hegemon', *Frankfurte Allgemeine Zeitung*, 21 April 2015.

of politics, which offered excellent training for the collaborative German leadership needed by the European Union as a whole.[5]

The Germans themselves had not wanted—still not did want—the hegemony that history had thrust upon them. The political elite shied away from it; voters were blind to it; intellectuals studiously avoided debating it. But the tasks before the country could not wait. The EU had yet to convert its (technocratic) output legitimacy into a (democratic) input legitimacy, and become a citizens' project. Powerful centrifugal forces were at work within it. Populist demagogy was rampant around Germany: it was enough to think of the Front National in France, Five Stars in Italy, Wilders in the Netherlands—even such northern bastions of sobriety as Sweden or Denmark were infected. With this contagion came refusal of any rational economic management, threatening the Stability Pact which Germany had steered through the Eurozone. To the South lay a Mediterranean that was ceasing to be a frontier, becoming once again, as of old, a sea that connected rather than separated its shores, as refugees poured across it into the Union. North Africa and the Levant—from Tunisia through Libya to Egypt and Syria—were all impinging upon Europe as never since the Dark Ages. In the world at large, the Union risked economic marginalisation if it continued to drift along with low growth rates, weak entrepreneurship, lack of innovation and absence of financial discipline.

Germany alone could provide, by example and by will, the leadership required to tackle these dangers. On it now depended the future of the EU: 'If Germany fails, Europe fails'.[6]

---

5   Even if, in the long run, alternation of government was no doubt a health certificate for democracy which it would be unwise to overlook: *Macht in der Mitte*, Hamburg 2005, pp. 165–7.

6   'Scheitert Deutschland an den Aufgaben der europäischen Zentralmacht, dann scheitert Europa': *FAZ*, 21 August 2015.

Its immediate tasks were two-fold: to become both 'pay-master and drill-master'—*Zahlmeister und Zuchtmeister*—of Europe. Germany was already the largest contributor to the budget of the Union, making over to it sums equivalent to the reparations imposed at Versailles, and its savers and consumers were paying for negative interest rates engineered by the Central Bank to encourage borrowing by profligate neighbours.[7] No one could say Germany was ungenerous. But in exchange, it had a right to insist that member states put their house in order, and to make sure that they did so.

Over and above all such contemporary considerations, it was an anthropological constant that all cultural and political systems of any dimensions required a centre. Historically, Jerusalem—Athens—Rome had fulfilled this need in the European imaginary. Today, by reason of its geographical location in the middle of the continent, bordering at once lands of Northern, Southern and Eastern Europe, that symbolic position fell to Germany. By ensuring that expansion of the EU to the North and East would counter-balance its earlier enlargement to the South, this was a position Berlin had sought, and should vigilantly safeguard against the danger of a Latin bloc taking shape against it, as proposed by Agamben in memory of Kojève. Germany should do its utmost to keep Britain within the Union as a healthy counterweight, to deter France from contemplating any such mischief. Geopolitical prudence required no less.[8]

Might all this lead to resentment, even fear of the new hegemon? That was not likely: Germans should not expect to be loved but respected, and sometimes admired. For Germany had one last, paradoxical advantage in the role it now had to assume. It was a 'vulnerable' hegemon because of its past.

---

7   *Macht in der Mitte*, pp. 178–80, 41–2, 146–7.

8   *Macht in der Mitte*, pp. 70–6, 28–9, 174–6.

The very criminality of the Third Reich had ensured that the Bundesrepublik would become the standard-bearer of democratic reliability in post-war Europe, and be perceived as such. Europeans could be confident that Germany would not abuse its power, as a country with a less guilty past might be tempted to do.[9] They had no reason to take fright at a little drilling for their own good. Ahead of them lay the common responsibility of Europe to bring order to its Großraum, as America became more focussed on its Pacific than its Atlantic flank. US power was withdrawing from the Mediterranean, the Black Sea and Baltic. In mustering collective resolve for the traditional tasks of policing the periphery, the new hegemon would also be needed. There Germany could not afford the abstention of its role in Libya: greater military strength, and willingness to use it in the common cause, were required.

In such postmodern imaginings of German paramountcy in Europe, time-worn tropes have reappeared. For Weber, the First World War was not willed by Germany, but thrust upon it, as a great power whose existence was an obstacle to other great powers: 'The fact that we are a people not of seven but of seventy millions—*that* was our fate. It founded an inexorable responsibility before history, which we could not evade even if we had wished'.[10] No longer confronting the Entente, but its weakling descendants, the same vocabulary has come back. The size of Germany condemns it to a responsibility—*Verantwortung*: no word is more frequent in the mouths of its politicians, from its pastor-President downwards—which it cannot evade, even if it wishes to, as it still continues to do. Such responsibility is a burden, as Kipling understood, and a painful one. Small wonder that, like the post-war America of Ikenberry's fond

---

9   *Macht in der Mitte*, pp. 168–70.
10   *Gesammelte politische Schriften*, Tübingen 1971, p. 143.

memory, post-Cold War Germany is reluctant to take it up: the country is being forced to become a hegemon against its will. For such tropes, Carr's judgment can be updated: in self-pity as self-praise, in the service of self-aggrandisement, power creates the pathos convenient to itself. Yet instructively: for nowhere on clearer display is the conceptual continuum between hegemony as consensual leadership of a federacy, as compellant predominance of one power over all others, and as natural sibling of empire, than in this current German discourse.

13

CONCLUSIONS

From pathos there is no better relief than the leading voices of dissent from American foreign policy in the United States itself. Of late, two of these stand out for their unsentimental realism, capable of coolly calling things by their name. In his major work *The Tragedy of Great Power Politics*, John Mearsheimer defined a hegemon as a state that is 'so powerful it dominates all the other states in the system. No other state has the military wherewithal to put up a serious fight against it'. Such hegemony, he argued, could never be more than regional, given that it was virtually impossible for any state to achieve global dominance because of the difficulty of projecting armed force across the world's oceans.[1] The United States was, and had long been, hegemon of the Western hemisphere, and it had always—as hegemons would—resisted, with success, the attempt of any peer rival to

---

1 *The Tragedy of Great Power Politics*, New York 2001, pp. 40–1. Christopher Layne, a fellow realist, has criticised the idea of the 'stopping power of water', arguing that on the contrary it is just because the US was protected by two oceans that it could aim at global hegemony by forward basing in Eurasia, as land powers in Eurasia could not hope to do in the Americas: 'The Poster Child for "offensive realism": America as a global hegemon': *Security Studies*, March 2009, pp. 12–128 ff. For a fuller, admiring but critical, discussion of Mearsheimer's variant of realism, see Peter Gowan, *New Left Review* 16, July–August 2002, pp. 47–67.

establish a comparable command of the Eastern hemisphere, at either end of Eurasia. After the end of the Cold War, however, despite enjoying all but impregnable security behind two oceans in its own domain, the US had in the permissive environment of unipolarity embarked on a reckless course of global dominance. This came in two versions: 'neo-conservative' under the younger Bush, and 'liberal imperialist' under Clinton and Obama, each plunging the country into a series of wars in regions of no strategic significance to it, at huge cost and to no end. At home, the drive for global dominance had undermined the rule of law, installing a mania for surveillance and contempt for due process.[2] Liberal imperialism was a dead end. It was time to withdraw to a saner stance of offshore balancing.

With no commitment to the stopping power of water, viewing the seas rather as a global commons whose command allowed just the retraction of US power that Mearsheimer recommended, Barry Posen of MIT could dispense with his regional proviso, and give liberal imperialism its appropriate synonym. His scathing work on recent American foreign policy opens with the simple, clinical sentence: 'The United States has grown incapable of moderating its ambitions in international politics.' For what reason? 'Since the collapse of Soviet power, it has pursued a grand strategy that can be called "Liberal Hegemony".'[3] That strategy is not a status quo policy: it is inherently expansionist. Its milestones have been the extension of NATO to the borders of Russia, the war in Kosovo and the war in Iraq—all elective blunders, compounded by the 'naïve and profligate' fashion in which the conflict in Afghanistan has been conducted. In all, it has kept the United States at war for nearly

---

2   'Imperial by Design', *The National Interest*, January–February 2011, pp. 16–34, and 'America Unhinged', *The National Interest*, January–February 2014, pp. 9–30.

3   *Restraint: A New Foundation for US Grand Strategy*, Ithaca 2014, p. xi.

twice as long as it was during the Cold War. The price of these adventures has been high. In real terms, by 2010 the financial cost of the war in Iraq alone was twice that of the Korean War, and exceeded that of the war in Vietnam, while a disorganised Iraqi nationalism had inflicted more proportional damage on US troops, as a ratio of combatant casualties, than highly organised Vietnamese nationalism had done. Huge sums that could have been invested in debt reduction or domestic infrastructure have been foregone.[4]

With what result? The attempt to build a functioning multi-ethnic democracy in the Greater Middle East had failed. No strong central government was achievable in Afghanistan. Iraq was engulfed in a chronic crisis of political violence. Ignoring the lessons of its own Civil War, the US had proceeded as if national, ethnic or religious identities were no obstacle to the imposition of its hegemonic will on foreign peoples. Confidence in modern high-technology weaponry had bred the illusion that 'military power is a scalpel that can be used to excise diseased politics', where in reality 'it remains a club, which in the end allows us to beat problems into a grudging submission at best, remission at worst'.[5] A rational grand strategy would cease all this, cutting military expenditure by half, and concentrating it on control of sea, air and space, in a policy of calculated restraint. But short of a major economic shock, there was little immediate prospect of this. 'US grand strategy is in the hands of a hugely self-confident, globally ambitious, and persistently self-replicating national security elite', lavishly endowed with intelligence and hardware resources, spanning Republican and Democratic parties alike. 'The Liberal Hegemony project will not be easily abandoned.'[6]

---

4   *Restraint*, pp. 25–6, 49–50, 58–9, 67.
5   *Restraint*, p. xiii.
6   *Restraint*, p. 173.

II

Across two millennia and more, the term has altered in usage and shifted in terrain, many times. Geographically, after its birth in classical Greece, hegemony travelled in different shapes to parliamentary Germany, Tsarist Russia, fascist Italy, Entente France, Cold War America, neoliberal England, retro-monarchist Spain, post-colonial India, feudal Japan, revolutionary China, and back to a subaltern Britain, aspirant Germany and unipolar United States. Politically, its theorists have at different times and places been liberals, conservatives, socialists, communists, populists, shields of reaction at one end, and swords of revolution at the other. But this has not been a random history, in which meanings bear little relation to each other as they move from one spatial or ideological emplacement to another. It has an intelligible pattern. From the beginning, there was a tension in the underlying connotations of hegemony. Leadership of a league: was that political or military? Were those led subjects or allies? Were its bonds voluntary or enforced? Every subsequent guise in which hegemony has reappeared has been haunted by the same ambiguity, however frequently—not invariably—those who have employed the notion have tried to banish it.

If hegemony were either just cultural authority or coercive power, the concept would be superfluous: there are many clearer names for each. Its persistence as a term is due to its combining of them, and the range of possible ways it can do so. Classically, it has always implied something more than simple might. That surplus has often become detached, as if exhausting its meaning. The reason is no mystery. In every age the language of politics is prone to euphemism, power sought or power obtained resisting any full exposure of itself. Reduced to a form of consensus, hegemony can lend itself to this, though a lingering sense that it may include another signification can make it suspect, as the oscillations and reservations that have marked its reception in the United States bear witness.[7]

Conjugation of the different planes of hegemony has been rare, and recent. Traditionally, and still in general actually, the history of national and international usages of the term has proceeded apart, the second structurally more liable to treat it in the register of compulsion rather than persuasion, by reason of the absence of any common authority in inter-state relations, other than the polite fictions of what passes for international law, observed only when advantageous to do so. The transnational plane of hegemony, by contrast the most purely cultural, remains least explored: so too the ways it is articulated with, and dependent on, the other two planes. At the base of the complex system they form, national hegemonies are, as Gramsci saw, the terrain where consent and coercion are typically in closest balance, whereas in the planes above them, one predominates, then the other.

With the globalisation of capital, these planes are becoming steadily more interconnected. For a symbolic illustration, it is enough to consider the award of the Nobel Peace Prize to the last president of the United States, within a year of his inauguration. The Prize itself, a million dollars in cash and countless more in publicity, belongs entirely to the transnational consumption of celebrity culture and commerce. At the national level, it burnished the image of the officeholder at entry to his tenure, for recycling through to his graceful exit. At the

---

7   As a liberal theorist of a 'democratic peace' puts it nervously: 'In contemporary discourse *hegemony* typically implies something tougher than the benign term "leadership", instead conveying a dominance in part exercised as overt or implicit coercion'; while 'in international politics' it is even 'not too far from the pejorative *empire*': Bruce Russett, *Hegemony and Democracy*, New York 2011, p. 1.

international level, its humble homage reminded the world of the continuing supremacy of the United States, and the fealty to it of even such an inconspicuous ally as Norway. At a time when his armies were occupying Iraq, escalating violence in Afghanistan, and raining fire on Pakistan, its president was awarded the West's highest distinction for work on behalf of humanity—benevolence, twenty-first century style. Gabriel García Márquez once remarked, viewing such earlier recipients of the award as Kissinger and Begin, that it would be better to call it by its real name, the Nobel Prize for War. The first ruler in American history to preside over uninterrupted military campaigns abroad across two full terms, Obama was entitled to that: at present, no less than seven wars, overt or covert, under his command, with further troops currently destined or dispatched where they were pledged to be withdrawn. This too is familiar from a classical past. In words that describe, as if they were written today, the journey from the 'audacity of hope' to the drones shattering villages of the Hindu Kush and the North-West Frontier, the Greek historian Diodorus Siculus, a contemporary of Julius Caesar, reported a judgment from the Ancient World on much the same combination of persuasion and coercion, ideology and violence, benevolence and *Schrecklichkeit*. In an enigmatic fragment that survives from his *Library of History,* perhaps recording a commentary on Roman operations in North Africa, he wrote: 'Those who wish to achieve hegemony acquire it with valour and intelligence (*andreia kai sunesis*), increase it with moderation and benevolence (*epieikeia kai philanthropōia*), and maintain it with fear and paralysing terror (*phobos kai kataplēxis*).'[8] The final term can stand for

---

8   XXXII, 2 (see also 4 on the sequence of Roman policies in Greece, North Africa and Spain, where *kataplēxanto* recurs). The fragment has attracted a considerable scholarly discussion, in part given the extent—wide, but

the last word of, at least, this hegemony. In the name of war on terror, war as terror, without boundary or end: *kataplēxis*, as far as the eye can see.

---

not complete—of Diodorus's reliance on Polybius as his primary source. The most detailed recent analysis argues that it must report the judgment of Greek observers at the time of the first Punic embassy to Rome in 150/151 BC as recounted in a lost passage of Polybius, though there are problems with the dating of this attribution: see Donald Baronowski, *Polybius and Roman Imperialism*, London 2011, pp. 106–13.

A SPECULATIVE POSTSCRIPT

In writing on the emergence of the term hegemony as a central notion in the Russian revolutionary movement at the turn of the twentieth century, independently of its adoption in the discourse of national unification in Germany in the mid-nineteenth century, which had lapsed by then, and with a meaning that was quite distinct from it, I was puzzled by the speed with which it became such a popular reference in the time of Nicholas II—well before it had any widespread political currency in Europe elsewhere—and the routes that could have made it so. A century later, queries in Russia produced no real answers. On mentioning this philological problem to my friend Anders Stephanson, he suggested a possibility. Mightn't it have arrived via the Greek New Testament, used for centuries by the Russian Orthodox Church, as distinct from its translation into Latin by the Roman rite? Sure enough, on checking the text, variants of hegemony, nominal and verbal, proved to be quite common—some twenty usages of *hēgemon* alone in Mark, Matthew, Luke and Acts, designating what the King James Bible and subsequent English versions would render as a 'governor', in contradistinction to a 'king'. Mark 13:9: ἐπὶ ἡγεμόνων καὶ βασιλέων σταθήσεσθε ἕνεκεν ἐμοῦ εἰς μαρτύριον αὐτοῖς—'you will stand before governors and kings for my sake to bear witness before them'. Matthew 27:2: καὶ δήσαντες αὐτὸν ἀπήγαγον καὶ παρέδωκαν Πιλάτῳ τῷ ἡγεμόνι—'when they had bound him, they led him away and delivered him to Pilate the governor'. Luke 3:1: Ἐν ἔτει δὲ πεντεκαιδεκάτῳ τῆς ἡγεμονίας Τιβερίου Καίσαρος, ἡγεμονεύοντος Ποντίου Πιλάτου τῆς Ἰουδαίας—'In the fifteenth year of the reign of Tiberius Caesar, Pontius Pilate being governor of Judaea'. Could clerical familiarity with such passages have filtered unobtrusively into secular culture? Such a conjecture might seem strained; though in local conditions, perhaps less improbable than appropriation from Thucydides.

INDEX